BUILDING BLOCKS BOOKS 2 AND 3

ISAIAH 58 MOBILE TRAINING INSTITUTE - STUDENT

ALL NATIONS INTERNATIONAL   AGNES I NUMER
GORDON SKINNER   ANNELLA WHITEHEAD

CONTENTS

Preface ix
Introduction xi
Living Isaiah 58 xv

15. Isaiah 58 — 1
    Review: Isaiah 58 — 17
16. Being Trained by The Spirit — 21
    Review: Trained by the Spirit of the Lord — 29
17. Natural and Spiritual Flow Together — 33
    Review: Natural and Spiritual Flow Together — 43
18. The Flow of God's Spirit — 47
    Review: The Flow of God's Spirit — 55
19. Ministering by the Spirit of the Lord — 59
    Review: Ministering by the Spirit of the Lord — 67
20. Christ in You the Hope of Glory — 69
    Review: Christ in You, the Hope of Glory — 77
21. God's Love Demonstrated — 81
    Review: God's Love Demonstrated — 93
22. Dwelling Together in Unity — 97
    Review: Dwelling Together in Unity — 107
23. Kingdom Authority — 111
    Review: Kingdom Authority — 127
    Review Key: Isaiah 58 — 131
24. Ezekiel's Wheel — 137
25. Revelation of Jesus Christ — 141
    Review: Revelation of Jesus Christ — 159
26. Mark - Face of the Ox — 163
    Review: Mark - Face of the Ox — 175
27. John - Son of God — 177
    Review John - Son of God — 189
28. Luke - Face of a Man — 191

Review: Luke's Gospel - the Face of a Man	203
29. Matthew - Face of the Lion	205
Review: Matthew - Face of the Lion	223
Review Key: Ezekiel's Wheel	225
About Isaiah 58 Mobile Training Institute	229

Building Blocks - Books 2 and 3
Isaiah 58 Mobile Training Institute
© 2016 All Nations International All rights reserved.
ISBN: 978-1-950123-33-9
Teresa Skinner Publishers

Unless otherwise indicated, all Scripture quotations are taken from the Holy Bible, King James Version - Public Domain. Scripture quotations marked (NLV) are taken from the Holy Bible, New Life version, copyright © Christian Literature International. Scripture quotations marked (ESV) ® Bible (The Holy Bible, English Standard Version®), © 2001 by Crossway, a publishing ministry of Good News Publishers. Used by permission. All rights reserved." Scripture quotations marked (Wuest) were taken from the New Testament and Expanded Translation by Kenneth S. Wuest © 1961 by the Wm. B. Eerdmans Publishing Co. Used by permission

Authors: Agnes I. Numer, Gordon Skinner, Teresa Skinner, Annella Whitehead, Kathy Vanzandt

Special Thanks: Veronica Sanchez
Editors: Julie Montague, Ashley Flores, Nona Babich, Chastity Carvel, Amber Lawton, Melanie Rodriquez, Joe Rodriguez, Virginia Russell, Kathy Vanzandt, Linda Vasquez **Transcribers:** Jennene Jeffrey, Kathy Vanzandt

Artwork: Julian Peter V. Arias, Cheryl Johnson, Jumi Sabbagh, Teresa Skinner, George Thomas, Adobe Stock, www.freepik.com
Cover Art: Julian Peter V. Arias and Eve Lorraine Rivers Trinidad

Isaiah 58 Mobile Training Institute books are available for use in training programs.
visit: is58mti.org
For more information or to order additional copies of this manual email: allnations@as.net contact us at www.all-nations.org
All Nations International PO Box 26632 Prescott Valley, AZ 86312

We dedicate this manual:
To those who wanted to know... but never had a teacher.
To those who looked for the vision... so that they could run with it.
To those who want to know "What's Next?"
To those who knew they were teachers... but did not know what to teach.
To those who are looking for Christ in Us the Hope of Glory!
May this manual reveal to you Jesus Christ and
May the peace that He has ordained for you be with you always.

PREFACE

As we travel around the world, we see pastors and leaders struggle with, "What to teach their people." Maybe they have never had Bible School training... and may never be able to afford it.

Our cry is that God will read this to you... that He will impart His Gospel to your heart, that He will train you, and that you will experience the freedom, peace power and ability to demonstrate His Love to the Nations.

May we all work together while there is time.... That He alone may be glorified.

Let Jesus take you to the Nations.....

> *"And this gospel of the kingdom shall be preached in all the world for a witness unto all nations; and then shall the end come."*
>
> — MATTHEW 24:14

Living Isaiah 58
Living a Fasted Life

In 1954, God gave Rev. Agnes I. Numer the revelation of Isaiah 58. He told her, "This is My plan, for My church, for the end of time." He showed her planes, trains, warehouses, training centers, centers of refuge, food distribution and so much more.

Rev. Numer established training centers where leaders received a vision, a hope, a plan and the principles of God's Kingdom. Those leaders passionately put these principles into practice in ministries around the globe. God has been their Jehovah Jireh.

God also showed Rev. Agnes I. Numer a school of ministry that would share these principles of His Kingdom to the nations.

Isaiah 58 Mobile Training Institute is available in print, eBook and online at isa58.org

> Thank you, All Nations International

Habakkuk 2:2 (KJV) "And the Lord answered me, and said, Write the vision, and make it plain upon tables, that he may run that readeth it. 3 For the vision is yet for an appointed time, but at the end it shall speak, and not lie: though it tarry, wait for it; because it will surely come, it will not tarry."

2 Timothy 2:2 (KJV) "And the things that thou hast heard of me among many witnesses, the same commit thou to faithful men, who shall be able to teach others also."

Rev. Agnes I. Numer, also known as the *"Mother Teresa of America"* passed away July 17, 2010 at 95 years of age. She has leaves behind a tremendous legacy.

LIVING ISAIAH 58

All Nations International, a church, and Sommer Haven Ranch International, a humanitarian aid non-profit, are two organizations founded and directed by Rev Agnes I. Numer who passed away July 17, 2010 at nearly 95 years of age. She left behind a tremendous legacy after 56 years of ministry. These ministries were birthed out of a revelation God gave her of Isaiah 58. When God showed her this revelation He told her, "This is My plan for My church for the end of time" The Lord showed her planes and trains, warehouses, training and refuge centers, a lot of food distribution and many other things.

It would be difficult to understand the impact this ministry has had over its more than 50 years existence. Almost as difficult as answering, "how many trees are in an apple seed" because that is what this international ministry has done... spread seeds. Many leaders have been given a vision, trained, developed, encouraged and supported. These leaders then have gone and have spawned many ministries around the world. They received a vision, a hope, a plan, and principles of God's Kingdom which work and then they passionately put what they had received into practice.

These international, ongoing ministries do not look to All Nations for financial support; they look to God. They have learned to know Him as Jehovah Jireh. And He provides for them because they are doing His work in His ways. In this training we will look at and hope to impart to you the principles they received which God has so greatly blessed. We give God all the glory. The training is by His Spirit to those who have an ear to hear, a heart to receive and a will to obey.

To Mention A Few Seeds That Have Sprung Up Into Trees Bearing Fruit

Don and Sandra Tipton founded and direct Friendships International. They have several ships traveling the globe bringing supplies where they are desperately needed. Their book *Jesus and Company*, shares the impartation Rev. Agnes Numer and the ministry of Sommer Haven has had in their lives.

Cliff Feldman, fed millions of people globally by the container loads and helped develop infrastructure that gave tilapia farms and poultry farms in South America.

Amy Wang, wrote a book sharing the impact that this ministry had on her life, had a million dollar church reaching the homeless and raising them up to be leaders. Her ministry is located just down the street from Los Angeles Union Rescue Mission. She traveled to China, Brazil, Tawain and many other countries declaring the Gospel of the Kingdom and raising up other ministries and leaders. Her son Pastor Gabriel Wang now carries her vision forward.

Patricia Capwell, director of Institute for Foundational Learning, was trained at Sommer Haven Missionary Training Center. She directs many low tuition schools in Asia. They have a staff of 50 full time workers and are nearly self-sufficient in food for their 150 residents on just over 10 hectares.

Native Americans trained under the ministry of Rev. Agnes I. Numer, are now leaders in their respective reservations throughout the United States. They are pastors of churches that they planted and built because of the transformation in their lives through her ministry.

Several works in India have been started and developed over the last 25 years. Orphanages, schools, clinics and churches have sprung up as a result. Just one of these ministries has ordained over 350 pastors. They all demonstrate the same Love of God as their mother ministry.

NEEPUganda, founded by Gertrude Kabatalemwa, provides livelihood for women and children, and schooling for many village children. Her son Emmanuel Mwesigye continues her ministry. They grow the majority of their own food which both feeds the children and teaches them agriculture.

Wells, grinding machines, large schools, peanut butter projects, chicken raising and agriculture projects have been done in Nigeria and are ongoing. One well project alone has made such an impact on the people of the area that there are now over 100 cell churches where there was only 10 in 2006. We now are building a training center in that area to prepare them to reach that entire area with the gospel of the Lord Jesus Christ and the love of God.

There is not time to mention the stories from Kazakstan, Mexico, Cambodia, Myanmar, China, Macao, Israel, Canada, Indonesia, Haiti and places we may have forgotten, but they have not forgotten that seed which they received.

During Disaster

When Mount Pinatubo erupted in the Philippines, our people were there and directly helped to rescue, relocate and rebuild the Aeta people who were natives to the slopes of the Mountain. Some of those Aeta people are staff members today.

During Katrina, All Nations joined with Friendships on one of their ships which traveled up the river to Gretna, which was completely cut off, bringing supplies, cooking for 10,000 people a day and supplying thousands of roofs with needed tarp material, nails and hammers.

Cliff Feldman was one of those who arranged thousands of semi loads directed towards New Orleans and Mississippi.

We will only mention the LA Riots, Tijuana Flooding, Chinese Refugees, 911, East Biloxi, Central India and others where God's love compelled us to respond to their needs with His Love, His Provision and His Glory.

Locally

Sommer Haven supplied an average of over 1/4 million pounds of food to 64,000 people a month for more than 35 years in the Antelope Valley, California through networking and training distributors.

Sommer Haven prepared groups as a Crisis response network ready to respond in case of a disaster in the Antelope Valley. These groups received and distributed food supplied by Sommer Haven every week and so are trained and ready to meet the needs of the community.

Training classes were conducted to raise up leaders who will start Community Garden Outreaches wherever God leads them.

All Nations continues to host International guests who come for training and also train groups and individuals from the United States who are preparing for missions. All Nations networks with other ministries who have the same heart and are willing to collaborate.

Chapter 15

ISAIAH 58

SINCE ALL NATIONS and Sommer Haven began with Agnes' revelation from God of Isaiah 58, let's look as this foundational scripture first. So many of the principles we lived by, without even calling them principles at the time, came from this powerful chapter. Please understand that we honor the whole word of God but He is the one who opened this particular chapter in an unusual way. He made it a central theme in our ministry.

The fast that God has not chosen

We all have a tendency to think that the way we serve God is right, that it is very pleasing to the Lord. It is hard for us to hear anything different, especially when our way seems so right to us and so many people agree with us. This may be the hardest area of our life for us to hear; when we are doing a "good" thing that is not totally a God thing. That is why Isaiah was told to:

Isaiah 58:1 Cry aloud, spare not, lift up thy voice like a trumpet, and show my people their transgression, and the house of Jacob their sins.

Isn't it very often true that we have to be shown something different in order to "see" where we are falling short? Let's look at where God's people in this chapter were missing it and see if this will help open our eyes to areas which are keeping us from having God's best. Let's take a minute to pray and open our hearts right now and ask God to help us, to be able to see.

The people in this chapter were seeking God daily, they were delighting to know His ways, they were asking God for right ordinances (ways or laws), and they were delighting in coming near to Him (feeling His presence).

Isaiah 58:2 Yet they seek me daily, and delight to know my ways, as a nation that did righteousness, and forsook not the ordinance of their God: they ask of me the ordinances of justice; they take delight in approaching to God.

They couldn't understand why even though they were seeking and fasting and afflicting their souls that God was not responding.

Isaiah 58:3 Wherefore have we fasted, say they, and thou seest not? wherefore have we afflicted our soul, and thou takest no knowledge?

God sent Isaiah to declare like a trumpet to them where they were falling short of pleasing God.

What are these things that Isaiah trumpeted?

In the day of your fast ye find pleasure.

- There is an "It's all about me" attitude we can get. Or worse yet, "look at me", or possibly, "what can

I get spiritually out of this fasting" Seeking God is not all about us. It is most importantly all about Him and what is on His heart. Our Father God loves us. He wants to meet with us and share His Heart with us and how He loves the broken people who need Him.

You still exact all your labors

- Some versions say this means, "you drive hard your workers" this sounds like no generosity on the job, with the workers, hardnosed in business matters, without mercy or compassion in business. God desires to flow into every area of our lives including how we do business.

You fast for strife and debate

- Our flesh loves to be spiritual, to be more spiritual than the next, even more powerful. There can be a lot of competition amongst God's leaders. The word of God is very honest about the shortcomings and strengths of its "heroes of faith". Pride and competition in our lives can show up even in our fasting.
- **James 4:1** From whence come wars and fighting among you? *come they* not hence, *even* of your lusts that war in your members?

You fast to smite with the fist of wickedness

- Could it be that some of them were doing the

equivalent of spiritual voodoo on other people? Wrong prayers can really affect God's people even when done ignorantly. If we don't love the people we are praying for we might not see things the way God does and we might not be praying according to His heart. This part is really not very pretty. These people were so determined they were right that they were willing to "fight for it"

- **Isaiah 58:4** ...Ye shall not fast as ye do this day, to make your voice to be heard on high.

We can also be pretty impressed with ourselves and our self-denial but God said he was not impressed by their self-afflicted religious rituals. Whatever is not done unto the Lord is sin. Jesus spoke against the practices of the Pharisees and Sadducees who loved religious rigors. (Please take the time to read Matthew 23) There is something in our flesh that loves these things but until we allow God to shine the light on these areas we will not be truly "heard on high"; we will still be thinking that we are doing great.

God asked, "Are you still going to call this a fast, are you still going to go on thinking this is an acceptable day unto the Lord?"

Isaiah 58:5 Is it such a fast that I have chosen? a day for a man to afflict his soul? Is it to bow down his head as a bulrush, and to spread sackcloth and ashes under him? <u>Wilt thou call this a fast</u>, an acceptable day to the LORD? Also see Zechariah 7:5

Isaiah 58 is often referred to as the "fasting chapter" and people go on long fasts based on this chapter. This misses the real point God is making, that just denying ourselves food, water or other things might not be what will reach the ear of God. It might not be this kind of fasting that will make the deepest heart changes we are seeking for in our own selves. What moves the heart of our Father? How can we "be heard on high"?

This is the Fast that I Have Chosen – Isaiah 58

There is another kind of self-denial that God makes very clear will be so pleasing to Him that He will hear our every whisper. There is a fast that He has chosen!

Break bands of wickedness

- If we live a fasted lifestyle, care more about the spiritual bondages and addictions of people than we care about ourselves, and allow Him to flow through us, He will break these bands. It is uncomfortable, inconvenient and unfamiliar to us but as we push past all that is uncomfortable we will find the Comforter supplying all of our needs and making up for all of our lacks. It is like walking on water.

Undo heavy burdens

- People carry many heavy things, sorrow, worry, guilt, poverty, debt, family concerns. God cares and He wants to care through us. When a family is going through a heavy situation we can be there with the Love of God to lift the heaviness.

Let the oppressed go free

- Demonic oppression, whether fear, torment,

suicide or violence can be broken as we become His representative. People came in to our ministry both day and night with a serious need to be set free. No matter what day or what time, if the Spirit of the Lord was moving we would move with Him, setting aside whatever else to minister to them. Many were set gloriously free. Each time we laid down our life for our "brethren" we also became more gloriously free.

Feed the hungry

- God cares, he provides, he wants to meet the needs of people who are hungry through us. Feeding the hungry is hard work, it is inconvenient; people will often be ungrateful; and not many people will notice us. It becomes a joy only when His love and Spirit are flowing through us. We have to set aside our flesh again and again and take up His anointing to touch needy people with His love, joy and grace. Our flesh will often rebel, complain and make excuses but as we press on deeper into the flow of His Spirit we will find life; His resurrection life. He hears this kind of fasting.

Clothe the naked

- Did you notice the hole in his shoe; did you see the little girl look down because she knows her clothes are torn? Can you see what God sees? Can you imagine the love they would feel if someone brought what they needed in such a demonstration of kindness that their lives would never be the same? Now that's fasting!

Bring outcast into your house

- One thing about the outcast is that nobody wants them… except for God. He died for them. Bringing these kinds of people into your house requires an extra grace that only comes when you begin to do it. It is likely not easy at first and there are a lot of inconveniences, and probably a little fear. If we set this aside He will love them through us. Oh! How quickly we will change.

Caring for your own flesh

- Ok, so we all know that sometimes the hardest people to love are our own family members. We can get so busy doing ministry or business that we overlook the ones closest to us. Can we minister the Love of God and can we see the needs of those in our own home? God did not miss this important balance to our lives in this chapter. Being a good Mom or a great big brother can really require denying ourselves. A little sister can be such a bug and just when we were ready to relax. Go ahead, deny yourself and love on her. Many pastors and ministers miss this part and suffer the results later in life. He will anoint you to love your family. You will have many who adopt you also. We have many teachers, many leaders but so few "Fathers" and Mothers.

Meet the needs of hungry and afflicted souls

- Hungry souls don't need our sympathy, they need His healing compassion, His loving kindness but they are often the most difficult people to love. They set up their walls of anger and rejection and will try to keep anyone from hurting them more. The very thing they need most is God's love "with skin on". Will we seek God until we have the wisdom, authority and grace to reach them? Will we travail until they are healed? This is pouring out our own soul to meet their needs. This is True Fasting.
- Hungry souls can be demanding and draining. It seems like they can never get filled up. We can only give what He gives us. Let us seek Him for more of a flowing of His ministry through us. They need Jesus through us.

STOP making yokes, putting forth the finger, and speaking vanity.

Yokes. Religious bondages that we wear and put on other people.

- **Matthew 23:4** For they bind heavy burdens and grievous to be borne, and lay them on men's shoulders; but they themselves will not move them with one of their fingers. Isaiah 10:1; Luke

11:46; Acts 15:10; But all their works they do for to be seen of men:

- Teachings, practices and policies might lead men to believe how great we are but they don't lead people to Jesus. They are yokes. Jesus came to set men free. He came to fulfill the law through loving God not through rules. People need a heart change that only comes by an encounter with God. **STOP** living by rules and enforcing them on others.

Fingers. Pointing accusingly at others. Fault finding, dishonoring.

When we **STOP** finger pointing and begin interceding for God to move in people's lives He will hear us. We will then begin to live a life of honoring, encouraging, building up, nurturing, serving.

Vain words. High sounding "Bible babble", platitudes, pat answers, religious formulas and clichés.

- What people really need is our transparency and God's compassion through us. We do not have all the answers. When we act like we do we offend people and God. He is the only answer and He will be the answer through us when we **STOP** vain words

Honor the Sabbath and delight in it by:

- Not speaking your own words. Delight to speak His words

- Not seeking your own pleasure. Delight to do His will
- Not finding your own ways. Delight to find His heart and know His ways

This is how Jesus lived.

John 5:19 So Jesus answered them, "I tell you the solemn truth, the Son can do nothing on his own initiative, **but only what he sees the Father doing.** For whatever the Father does, the Son does likewise.

John 12:49 For I have not spoken of myself; but the Father which sent me, he gave me a commandment, what I should say, and what I should speak

John 17:8 For I have given unto them the words which thou gavest me

We might not mind doing God's will if we can do it our own way

There is a Sabbath rest that we can enter into. Hebrews 4 says that some must enter even though they did not enter in because of their grumbling and their unbelief. Do we trust Him when our ability is drained or do we complain? When things begin to look bad can we declare His word into the situation and just rest?

Hebrews 4:9 There remaineth therefore a rest to the people of God. 10. For he that is entered into his rest, he also hath ceased from his own works, as God did from his.

There is a place in God where we are doing His works in His Strength. We begin to have a river flowing through us that also gives us rest even for our bodies, but first we must **STOP** our own laboring. God can train us if we ask Him.

Now... We Begin to Build with God... Bringing His Kingdom to Earth

Isaiah 58:12-14

Build the old waste places

- The enemy comes to steal, kill and destroy but Jesus came to give us life more abundantly. That abundant life in us begins to "make all things new". Places which have both spiritually and naturally been laid waste for generations will be built up through people filled with His Spirit and His Kingdom. He knows how to take waste places and make them a fruitful garden.
- **Isaiah 51:3** For the LORD shall comfort Zion: he will comfort all her waste places; and he will make her wilderness like Eden, and her desert like the garden of the LORD; joy and gladness shall be found therein, thanksgiving, and the voice of melody.
- We have experienced so many times when we went to an area in great need, and cleaned and repaired in the natural, that God brought freedom in the spiritual realms.

Raise up the foundations of many generations

- People, families and communities are broken to their very foundations. Usually there is a long history of traumatic events that have rent the fabric of their society. They often carry an identity of victims and not victors. These foundations of lives and communities can be raised up again through the people of God. They can again have a firm foundation and a new identity on which to build which is based on forgiveness, reconciliation and restoration.

Repair the breaches

- Breaches are broken gaps in a stone wall which allows free access to predators and enemies. Sometimes we call them "open doors for the enemy". If people are believing lies they will be easy targets. Psalms 91:4 Thy Truth is a shield and buckler (both used for protection from enemies). When people are missing principles of God's Kingdom they have gaps. Can we let Jesus in us fill in those gaps with Truth so people can stand in freedom?

Restore the paths to dwell in

- A path is made from many feet going where they often go. It is the habits of a people; everyday life. Where they live and how they live every day. For many people, there was once a path that their people dwelled in but they lost their way; like many of our dear Native Americans. For other people, It is hard to live without enough food, water, or resources. The 3 mile hike for water every morning to the muddy river in Nigeria

made a path. The large commercial well which now serves over 10,000 people has shortened that path and the water doesn't make them sick. They now know there is a God in heaven that cares about them.
- Restoring broken people, families, villages and communities is close to Father God's heart. Poor Health and nutrition shortens the path of a mother's life, her children will have to raise themselves. For people to live and thrive Jesus wants to bring them agriculture, sanitation, clean water, health and hygiene, small businesses, education, and community development.
- **Psalms 16:11** Thou wilt show me the path of life: in thy presence is fullness of joy; at thy right hand there are pleasures for evermore.
- **Psalms 23:3** He restores my soul: he leads me in the paths of righteousness for his name's sake.
- God wants a people who can live in His presence and walk in His ways of righteousness and bring His Kingdom to "all tribes and peoples and tongues".

Light, Health, Righteousness, Glory: This is the heritage of the People of Isaiah 58

Isaiah 58:8 Then shall thy light break forth as the morning, and thine health shall spring forth speedily: and thy righteousness shall go before thee; the glory of the LORD shall be thy rereward. **9** Then shalt thou call, and the LORD shall answer; thou shalt cry, and he shall say, Here I am. then shall thy light rise in obscurity, and thy darkness be as the noonday:

Isaiah 58:11 And the LORD shall guide thee continually, and satisfy thy soul in drought, and make fat thy bones: and thou shalt be like a watered garden, and like a spring of water, whose waters fail not.

Isaiah 58:14 Then shalt thou delight thyself in the LORD; and I will cause thee to ride upon the high places of the earth, and feed thee with the heritage of Jacob thy father: for the mouth of the LORD hath spoken it.

- God declares through Isaiah that we will be like a watered garden, fully satisfied and never dry.
- God declared we would be delighted in Him, He would guide us continually: We will never lack for His good direction.
- God declared that we would be full of light like mid-day. That we would rise up and our light would be seen by many. (read **Isaiah 60**)
- God said that He would feed us with what He promised Jacob.
- God said then we would ride on the high places of the earth… with Him

His own mouth declared prosperity, blessing, favor in high places, favor with God, and spiritual experiences with God. All God really means by this can only be reached by learning to go lower and serve better and love stronger and believe more… FOR OTHERS

For the Mouth of the Lord Has Spoken It

This is one chapter that the Lord personally "signed" His Name to.

This phrase is only used 4 times in the entire bible. These promises are endorsed by Him.

All Heaven stands behind these words to perform them.

Let's Review:

REVIEW: ISAIAH 58

1. The prophet Isaiah had to lift up his voice like a trumpet because:
a. People lived far apart
b. They could not hear what God was saying to them
c. They lived in the mountains
d. Their neighbors played loud music

2. God will always hear us when we fast, seek His face and worship
a. True
b. False

3. "You fast for strife a debate refers to:
a. Ungodly business practices
b. A "look at me" attitude
c. Pride and competition between God's leaders
d. Being willing to fight to be right

4. How are Bands of wickedness broken?
a. Living a fasted lifestyle

b. Praying Louder and longer
c. Lifting weights
d. Sitting in ashes and wearing sackcloth

5. Feeding the hungry in Is 58:6 is means to give people spiritual food like preaching
a. True
b. False

6. Caring for your own flesh means
a. Brushing your teeth before meeting people
b. Taking care of your own family with God's love
c. Having sympathy for people
d. Getting enough sleep at night

7. We can honor the Sabbath by
a. Not eating on that day
b. Attending several church services
c. Delighting to do His will and speak His words
d. Resting extra on that day

8. Doing deeds of kindness in practical ways can have great spiritual results
a. True
b. False

9. what are breaches?
a. small insects in the water
b. leather straps which attach a warriors armor
c. boldly colored circles used for target practice
d. gaps of truth in people's lives which allow access to enemies

10. Restoring the Paths to Dwell in
a. Upgrading roads so people can travel easily
b. Helping broken families and communities to recover and thrive
c. Building houses on the main roads
d. Installing new stop signs for safety

11. Raise up the Foundations of many generations can mean
a. Building new homes for people
b. Giving people a new identity on which to build their future
c. Teaching truths which fill in spiritual gaps
d. Giving your children a good education

12. Bringing God's Kingdom to a village involves only the spiritual truths and principles.
a. True
b. False

13. In this chapter when we deny our own selves to love others God promises that
a. We will become rich
b. We will be the greatest in His Kingdom
c. We will become like a fruitful garden. Never dry
d. We will have the newest vehicle we claim

14. Isaiah 58 Fasting Releases all that God promised to Jacob
a. True
b. False

15. Who singed his name to the promises in this chapter?
a. Jeremiah
b. Joel
c. God
d. Isaiah

Chapter 16
BEING TRAINED BY THE SPIRIT

Learning to hear the voice of the Lord

AGNES WOULD OFTEN COMMENT, "It is not difficult to hear the voice of the Lord, all you have to do is **get the junk out of your life**. You have too many other things going on in your head". She also would tell us to, "take those things out of your ears. God wants to speak to you but how can He with that music always going on?"

The world, the flesh, the devil and all of the people around us are speaking to us and projecting messages to us but **we can learn** in the middle of anything that might be going on to hear His still small voice. He knows the way and He loves to speak to His children.

The only one who can train us is the Spirit of the Lord. If we can learn to hear and trust God's voice then He can direct us in almost any direction but we must be trained to hear, learn and obey. There are a lot of attitudes, distractions and resistances in our lives that keep us from being open to what is on His heart. These must be surrendered to Him and changed by Him. This is a process. **This is TRAINING.**

Take Everything As Training

We can fight the work of the Holy Spirit in our lives if we like but it just makes the process longer and more difficult. If we could only learn to trust Him, yield to Him and cooperate with what He is doing in our lives. If we could really understand that he is forming us for a particular purpose so we can bring Glory to God, then we could cooperate with Him, even joyfully. See James 1:2-4.

We can decide that from now on we are going to take everything that happens to us as training. No matter what it is! We can trust that He will not test us above what we are able. We can be confident that He is doing a good thing in our hearts since He can only do good things. We can know that if we completely give our lives into His service that He will accept us and begin right away **TRAINING US.**

Why not pray a prayer of surrender and commitment right now. Why not invite the Holy Spirit to have His way in you. Why not decide that from now on, no matter what happens you are going to take it for training. Why not declare right now, "I am being trained to be an awesome minister of God's love and His Glory"

The Process of Tempering God's People

Agnes ministered often about the old steel mill just across the river where her family lived in Ohio. She would describe the bright fiery light and how they would melt away the impurities of the steel with intense heat then douse it with water. The process would continue with forming that steel into beams which would be able to endure the stresses of carrying cars across long bridge spans for years without breaking. Those beams had to be tempered correctly so they would not bend or crack under the weight.

Blacksmiths pound steel into various shapes when enough heat has been applied to the metal to nearly melt it. Many areas of our lives require the expert TRAINER, the Holy Spirit to place us in some hotspots until we are about ready for a meltdown. It is then He can form us into the instrument in His hand which is suited for His work. But we are not ready yet. He then douses us in cool oil or fresh water to get just the right amount of tempering. All of this process is at the hands of an expert. We must learn to trust that He knows what He is doing and we are in His hands.

Getting the Junk Out Of Your Life

OK, now that we have surrendered to the Holy Spirit and have decided to take everything for training and we understand a little about the process; let's get started. We love the Lord and enjoy the worship but these people get under my skin... oops the training has begun in earnest. "Oh no, I didn't know God was going to use people!" "Do you mean I have to work with him?" Yes, every person around us we need to learn to love, be kind to and get along with. This works His nature into us. We cannot do it alone. What is in us is selfish and self seeking but He knows how to expose this and remove it.

We love to blame **that** person for being so unlovely but if we take everything for training we will have to admit that **we** have "**junk**" in that area. We have to accept more grace and more of His love. Let God deal with **that** person; you let Him change you until you are free and can love them. Then you can begin to minister to them.

What is Junk? It is sin, the old Adamic nature, habits, poor character, curses in our lives, things we inherited, wounds that haven't been healed, lies we believe, wrong thinking, nasty attitudes, prejudice, rebellion, resistance, flesh, impurities, stubbornness, grumpiness, lust, anger, even murder or suicide, etc., etc., etc.

We all have it. We all tend to hide it just like Adam and Eve. We all see it in others better than in ourselves. We all can be free if we want to. The dear Holy Spirit and Fire will help us GET THE JUNK OUT of our lives and he will use people and circumstances.

Bring It to the Light So It Can Be Removed

When we purpose in our own self to become a vessel of honor, we take a stand on the side of God against all dishonorable things. God who is wants to clean us up will be happy to cleanse us. As the Holy Spirit exposes those things in us we begin to SEE OUR OWN JUNK. In fact He will make our junk so obvious to us and others that we can no longer deny it even if we struggle. Once we begin to view the JUNK as our enemy and we fall out of agreement with it, those things are no longer our "friend". In fact we can even **bring it to the light**. This means we confess it to someone and God can remove it. He wants to remove it and He will just as soon as **we** are ready.

2 Timothy 2:21 If a man therefore purge himself from these, he shall be a vessel unto honour, sanctified, and meet for the master's use, and prepared unto every good work. (i.e. useful to the Master in many ways)

One device in our lives that keeps us from "bringing things to the light" is Shame. People will hide their sins for years and the devil will torment them with it and keep them in bondage. Shame is fear. It is based on a lie. The lie is something like, "If they ever found out…" or "I could never admit that someone such as I could ever have…." (which is pride) We are in fact all broken sinners saved by His Grace.

In our community of people we wanted to help each other become free. Once we had tasted the joy of freedom we were really ready to cooperate with the Holy Spirit. Also, once we learned that we could trust each other without losing honor we all became free a lot faster. There is no fear in love. Perfect love casts out fear. Once we come to love each other with His love we can help each other. There is no shame if you set yourself against the enemy.

There is a beautiful picture in the marriage preparations made by a bride and her maids. They all are working together, planning, preparing, and helping one another to become ready. Everything must be clean and new. No spot can remain. They laugh and talk and work on one another's hair and faces. If the body of Christ could help each other to become ready with this same spirit how quickly we could become clean and useful to our Master.

Other Lords besides God

None of us had any hope of living for God and bringing His Love and His Glory to other people in need because we were so messed up ourselves. Some of us had been tormented and possessed since we were young. We had committed every kind of sin and had nearly every kind of bondage that the devil could bring. When Agnes first ministered this scripture such amazed joy and hope sprung up in us all. "You mean we can have peace? We can be free?" "God, you would work in us all your works? WOW"

Isaiah 26:12 LORD, thou wilt ordain peace for us: for thou also hast wrought all our works in us. **13** O LORD our God, other lords beside thee have had dominion over us: *but* by thee only will we make mention of thy name. **14** *They* are dead, they shall not live; *they* are deceased, they shall not rise: therefore hast thou visited and destroyed them, and made all their memory to perish.

That part, "and made all their memory to perish" was the most amazing part of all. How could it be that these things that had held us bound every day for years and years could be broken? Could we really be so free that we would not even remember how we once were? This was an awesome revelation, and thrilling.

Whatever your doctrine about us having other "Lords" in us besides God we knew those Lords were there and the word had come that we could be free. God VISITED those other demonic Lords. They died, they were deceased so that we would truly have "no other gods besides Thee" No other Lords would any longer have dominion over us.

Dead means no longer living. Deceased means dead, buried and got the death certificate. It means "no longer at this address" It means you can't even find him anymore.

The Spirit of Judgment and the Spirit of Burning

When the Holy Spirit would help expose an area in our life and we would "bring it to the light" He would then come with the Spirit of Judgment and of Burning and deal with the devil and his works and consume the flesh and its works.

Isaiah 4:3 And it shall come to pass, that he that is left in

Zion, and he that remains in Jerusalem, shall be called holy, even every one that is written among the living in Jerusalem: 4 When the Lord shall have washed away the filth of the daughters of Zion, and shall have purged the blood of Jerusalem from the midst thereof by the spirit of judgment, and by the spirit of burning.

Judgment to the devil and His Works

John 14:11 Of judgment, because the prince of this world is judged. John 12:31; John 14:30; Eph 2:2; Col 2:15;

We have made covenants with the devil and oaths within our own selves which bind us up. A dishonest used car salesman will get you to sign a contract which is unfair and deceptive because he knows you really want that flashy car, and by law you still have to "pay all". God comes and breaks these unfair and deceptive covenants we have made if we will renounce them.

Burning to the Works of the Flesh

It is the heat of the fire that refines the metal until it is pure. "He shall baptize you with the Holy Ghost and fire", said John the Baptist. How much we need this cleansing fire to prepare us to be ministers of His Glory. Oh, how much the world needs to see people who have overcome the flesh to give them hope. Under John the Baptist lives were changed as they repented and became baptized but John knew that they still needed, "He that cometh.. will baptize you with the Holy Spirit and with Fire." Matthew 3:11, Luke 3:16

Our God is a Consuming Fire. In His love, His presence,

His holiness, we become undone. He transforms us into His own image from Glory to Glory by the fire of His presence.

One of the Keys of His Kingdom is being trained by Him to hear His voice. He said, "My sheep hear my voice and another they will not follow". It is natural to hear His voice and to be led by Him. Paul said, "as many as are led by the Spirit, these are the sons of God." As He makes us free and sets up His reign in our hearts He begins to train us to do the will of the Father even as He did while on earth. He will lead us through a process that prepares us to trust Him in all things. We will become unshakable as He shakes everything that can be shaken. He will form His Kingdom in us and then take us to the world so He can demonstrate His Love through us.

Did you invite the Holy Spirit to have His way in you? Did you decide that from now on, no matter what happens you are going to take it for training? Are you practicing bringing things to the light? Why not declare again right now, "I am being trained to be an awesome minister of God's love and His Glory"

REVIEW: TRAINED BY THE SPIRIT OF THE LORD

1. What is the key to hearing the voice of God clearly?
a. Listening to soft music
b. Memorizing scripture verses
c. Let Him deal with attitudes, distractions and resistances in our lives
d. Wearing hearing aids

2. What we might be doing which can cause the training process to be longer
a. Fighting or resisting the work of the Holy Spirit in our lives
b. Trusting fully in God's word
c. Being fully surrendered to His dealing
d. Taking everything that happens as training

3. We can accept that even difficult people who we meet can be used for our training.
a. True
b. False

4. Tempering is a word which is used to describe:
a. Getting very angry
b. When Satan puts distraction in our path
c. How diamonds are formed in the earth
d. The process of making steel strong so it will not bend or break

5. What is one way which God uses to develop His love in us?
a. Listening to deep biblical teachings
b. Sending difficult people into our lives]
c. Paying your tithes regularly
d. Celebrating your birthday

6. Find the best definition of Junk in our lives
a. The old Adamic nature
b. Habits and poor character traits
c. Lies and wrong thinking
d. All of the above

7. When the Holy Spirit helps us to see our own junk then we should
a. Open a new bank account
b. Feel shame and sorrow
c. Bring it to the light
d. Deny that we have an issue and confess that we are already made perfect

8. What will God do to our Former Lords that had dominion over us?
a. Restore them to their rightful place
b. Visit them "and made all their memory to perish"

c. Keep them waiting until the final judgement
d. Make them read the whole book of Genesis

9. The "Spirit of Judgement" refers to:
a. Getting angry at a brother who has done you wrong
b. How God deals with the devil and his works in our lives
c. The White Throne Judgement in the Last Days
d. How we become free from the works of our flesh

10. The "Spirit of Burning" refers to:
a. Hell fire and brimstone reserved for the devil and his angels
b. The loving fire of the Holy Spirit which he brings to purify our flesh
c. How God deals with the devil and his works in our lives
d. The process of removing old covenants and deception we have made with Satan

Chapter 17

NATURAL AND SPIRITUAL FLOW TOGETHER

NOT MANY PEOPLE expect a spiritual training center to have their people doing so many natural things but so much of the training we received by the Spirit of the Lord was while we were busy washing dishes, feeding the hungry, pruning the orchard, building a cabin, feeding the animals etc. If we can hear His voice in the little things He can speak to us about spiritual things as well.

We, at Sommer Haven, remember so well the times when we would all be doing our various tasks and we would feel a sudden travail in our spirit. One by one we all would find our way to the living room where our meetings were held and soon most of us would be there. As we shared we discovered that we all felt the same thing. When we would begin praying God would move. We were all hearing from Him. If one of us would miss coming in, we would feel sad that we had missed His voice and ask Him to help us learn to be more sensitive the next time.

Everything You Do, Do Unto the Lord.

Once we have determined to take everything that happens in our life for training and have opened our heart to hear His voice in the Natural things then we learn to do everything we do, UNTO THE LORD

Faithful in the little – ruler over much

Luke 19:17 And he said unto him, Well, thou good servant: because thou hast been faithful in a very little, have thou authority over ten cities.

Matthew 25:21 His lord said unto him, Well done, thou good and faithful servant: thou hast been faithful over a few things, I will make thee ruler over many things: enter thou into the joy of thy lord.

The little things do not appeal to the flesh so much. There is not much glory in them, not many people will notice us, but faithfulness in the little things brings the kind of character God can use. Simple duties often repeated "as unto the Lord" yields great spiritual progress, obedience and humility.

Despise not the day of small things.

- God's little impression in our spirit can easily be overlooked. The thing He is putting in our heart is not a big thing at all and to us it does not even seem to be important. That is the way He began with us, a little nudge to do a small thing but God was in the middle of it and He knew where He was leading. Soon that very little thing led to an amazing open door for ministry.
- If we are looking to start a big ministry we may be on our own to build it; but if we let Him make us faithful and obedient to do whatever we hear

from Him with a faithful heart. As we learn to do it unto Him then He can build something big in us and through us. We just have to be faithful in what He has given us today.
- I have chosen the weak things of this world....
- It is easy to discount ourselves as qualified for what God is asking because we know we are weak. After the Holy Spirit has worked in us for a while we realize just how inadequate we really are. This is just the place that the Lord can begin to use us. We now have to learn that it is very OK to be weak, for in our weakness He is made strong. We will now have to learn to let Him be GREAT through us.
- Moses felt inadequate, Gideon felt insignificant, Isaiah felt unclean, but God had chosen every one of them for great things.
- Agnes often quoted, "Little is much when God is in it. Much is little when He's not there".

What is In Your Hand?

Begin with what you have... Just begin

Once Agnes had received the revelation of Isaiah 58 where she saw planes and trains and semi-trucks and warehouses and all of those big things she began by taking one small cupboard in her house and filling it with food that she bought using a small monthly check that came from her brother's death in the war. Any time she found a family in need she would go to that cupboard and give. Agnes and her son, David had gardens that grew well. There were always a few eggs and some garden produce to give as well.

When Agnes began to share her vision she said, "And we

will have semi-trucks coming up and down this driveway". We did not wait for the semi-trucks to arrive before we started. We had an old red pickup truck so that is where we began. At first we travelled all the way to Los Angeles and picked up a couple of boxes of food. That food was not much good, by the time we sorted through it there was not much left. "But God trained us", Agnes would tell, "He trained us in the little things, He trained us not to waste, we learned how to use every little thing and make it a blessing"

Soon we were going to the local markets and farmers and they began to give. Agnes also tells the story how that one day "one of the young men was going down a country road looking for hay for our animals and a woman and her son were walking down this road. And the Lord said, "Stop and talk to them." And so he stopped and began to talk. The mother couldn't speak English but the little boy could. Her husband had just had heart surgery and was disabled and very, very ill, and they didn't have any food. So we fixed them some food. The Lord delivered them from alcoholism and this family became our greatest distributors of food giving to 350 families in this valley. It began with a little food box."

A simple nudge/impression not a huge revelation

"Sometimes it's just a little nudge – just a little thing – and we want to shove it aside and say, well, it's not important. We don't realize how important it is until we pay attention to it. Then we begin to see it expand and expand, and God begins to enlarge it, and it becomes a great thing that He would have us to do." (Rev. Agnes Numer).

We often miss it because it is not big enough for us

How many people miss what God wants to do because they are "way up there somewhere" prophesying and evangelizing? How many people overlook the Father's heart for the least and the lost? We have sadly seen many "big" ministers who step over the "unimportant little people" on their way to the stage. Jesus would have stopped to heal them. He said, "I came for those who are sick" Are you aiming to "have a ministry" or to minister?

1 Corinthians 1:27 But God hath chosen the foolish things of the world to confound the wise; and God hath chosen the weak things of the world to confound the things which are mighty;

God blesses simple obedience

Just because it is a good idea doesn't mean it is a God idea. "Obedience is better than sacrifice" When we learn to be led by the Spirit of God we will be called the SONS of God. This is not referring to baby sons. This is meaning mature ones who are able to join with the Father in the Father's business. We become coworkers with our Father. We become Sons through simple obedience. We learn obedience through the little and the big things; through the hard and the mundane; through the big responsibilities and the small, faithful ones. Jesus obeyed His Father in all things and only did what He saw his Father do.

Hebrews 5:8 Though he were a Son, yet learned he obedience by the things which he suffered;

See a Need and Do It

Learn His voice in the natural.

When we are putting together a box of food for a family, it is individualized to meet the needs of those people. We don't know them but God knows them and He wants to let them know just how much He loves them. He directs us just what to put in each box. It is common to hear the Oooo's and Ahh's and "Wow I love that cereal" and "how did you know our Dad is diabetic?" We didn't know but He knows and that little small voice that we know and love would nudges us this way or that. Often you can "just know" what item should be in that box. You could feel His pleasure if you will learn to listen in the natural things.

If You See the Need Ask Him for the "How To"

Praise God that you are becoming more sensitive to the needs around you. Praise God, you saw that need; but now what. There is no way you can meet it and you are tempted to wish you never saw it because now you feel bad. No, don't think that way. The same God who opened your eyes to see the need can make the provision to meet it also. He can use that opportunity to show HOW GREAT HE IS.

So often we experienced seeing some items come into the ministry and no one had any idea what we were going to do with them. But we would say, "Lord, you have provided it, please show us what it is for". Even the same day sometimes, a person would come in who needed those very things.

At other times the need came first and then we would see the provision. One of us might be praying for a comb or a hairbrush, or a certain kind of toothpaste and there it would be tucked away in a box of donations. If we were not sensitive we might not realize that someone had been praying for this item and we might use it in another way. But as we learned to flow by His Spirit everything would work out in the most amazing and exciting ways.

We can simply know that if He moves on our heart to see a need that He is the one who wants to meet that need. If we are willing He will often bless us to be the one to meet that need. And then we get the joy of seeing Him move.

When we learn this principle in everyday life, in the natural realm, we can move with Him into bigger things. It is the same principle, **see a need and move with Him to do it**.

A Good Steward

Here we are now. We are learning to know Jehovah Jireh. God is beginning to pour in the blessings and the ministry is expanding, more people are coming to volunteer and our responsibilities are growing. Here is another part of our training. Can we learn to be a good steward over the blessings of the Lord and the people He sends? If we are able to learn to be a good steward where we are now, He can use us in greater things. Will we allow Him to train us in this area as well?

Faithfulness

The key to leadership is faithful followership. A person who is loyal and faithful to what God has entrusted to his care will be blessed by God. When we do everything as unto the Lord and not unto man (as men pleasers), then HE will see our faithfulness and reward us. God loves to reward us. He is more willing to give than we are ready to receive.

1 Corinthians 4:2 Moreover it is required in stewards, that a man be found faithful.

Luke 12:42 And the Lord said, "Who then is that faithful and wise steward, whom his lord shall make ruler over his household, to give them their portion of meat in due season?"

Thank God that the faithfulness that is in us is His Son.

Christ in Us. When we are tempted to cut corners, and we think, "my Master is taking so long to promote me that I am going to take it easy. He said that when He would come I would get blessed and now it has been way too long. I am going to just bless my own self right here". Don't give into that temptation. This is the very test of FAITHFULNESS that you must pass before God will bless. Call upon the Lord to give you more of His faithfulness, more of Jesus nature in you. He is called "Faithful and True" (Rev 19:11)

Waste

When God has provided many blessings into our hands it takes a Holy Spirit diligence to make sure that those things are not wasted. One time we were given 78 pallets of green bananas (that's 156,000 pounds). Green bananas cannot be eaten until they ripen. Every box had to have a ripe banana put inside of it to help ripen the rest. Then as the bananas began to get ripe, all of the plastic liners had to be removed from each box or they would turn to mush. We hand sorted each of those boxes at least 3 times, turning each box over, opening it and restacking it on another pallet. We only lost half of one pallet that was not given out as a blessing out of all of those 78 pallets.

Luke 16:1 And he said also unto his disciples, There was a certain rich man, which had a steward; and the same was accused unto him that he had wasted his goods. (Read what happens to that steward)

If we are not found faithful, that which we have will be taken away

Over Another Man's Goods

A steward is someone who is in charge of **another man's goods**. He is required to manage his things and his people just the way the owner would have done it. If he does he will hear, "well done my good and faithful servant". If not he may hear, "depart from me".

We are not our own and even what we have has been given. God wants to give us much but we have to learn the principles of stewardship.

Luke 16:12 And if ye have not been faithful in that which is another man's, who shall give you that which is your own?

We will usually start "our ministry" under the authority of "another man's ministry". We will not be entrusted by God with our own ministry if we cannot be faithful where we are. If we can be an excellent steward God will bring the increase.

1 Corinthians 10:24 Let no man seek his own, but every man another's wealth.

God will set us under tutors for our training. We can take the experience of even a poor tutor and allow it to train us. Because, remember, we are being TRAINED BY THE SPIRIT OF THE LORD and not a man. We can take even this for training if we can maintain a correct attitude. Can we allow Him to give us the Grace for each day and each person we meet?

Will We Consume it On Ourselves?

When men begin to praise us will we soak it up? When they are saying how great we are will we tell them the truth that we are just broken people mended by grace? Will we be honest that "No good thing dwells in me"? (Rom. 7:18)

1 Peter 4:10 As every man hath received the gift, even so minister the same one to another, as good stewards of the manifold grace of God.

We have to remember that the glory belongs to God and not to another. (Acts12:23) The Holy Spirit will train us to be careful to give Him the Praise.

Remember this little test. "If you grumble when things go wrong you will gloat when they prosper". Just **you** be a faithful steward unto the Lord.

Have an Ear to Hear, a Heart to Receive, and a Will to Obey

God can take each and every natural event and use it for our training. We are being trained to hear His voice and flow by His Spirit. We are learning that God uses the ordinary things to bring out the extraordinary qualities of His nature in our lives.

Can we learn to remain in His presence in the middle of adversity? Can we learn to love the unlovely? Can we stand in His truth when others are deceived? Do we know how to call upon Jehovah Jireh when there is a need? Can we continue faithful when it seems He is "tarrying"? Can we give Him all the glory when he prospers us? Will we stand for purity in the midst of a perverse world? Let us allow Him to remove the junk from our lives so we can be TRAINED TO FLOW BY HIS SPIRIT?

REVIEW: NATURAL AND SPIRITUAL FLOW TOGETHER

1. We can learn to hear God's voice by
a. Ignoring everything around you and singing hymns
b. Praying all day
c. Letting God train you in the natural things
d. Always trying to be perfect

2. If you are going to start a big ministry you have to learn
a. Church organizational structure
b. Learn to be faithful and obedient in the little things He gives you
c. Getting on to the radio so you are heard by many people
d. Become as powerful a speaker as you can be

3. When God gives you a large vision for ministry
a. Share with everyone how God is going to use you
b. Gather many influential people around you
c. Create a budget and wait until you have the finances
d. Just begin with what you have in your hand. Let God bring the increase

4. We can miss the simple nudge of the Holy Spirit because we are waiting for a great revelation
a. True
b. False

5. When you have a big ministry you do not need to associate with the little people
a. True
b. False

6. An important key to developing good leadership is:
a. Know how to give clear instructions
b. The ability to let people know who's boss
c. Being a faithful follower first
d. Having a great personality

7. We can be faithful because The Faithful One lives in us
a. True
b. False

8. If we are not faithful even that which we have will be taken away
a. True
b. False

9. Most God inspired ministries start
a. With a might revelation
b. Under another man's ministry
c. In Bible School
d. With a bang, suddenly

10. God often uses broken people mended by grace

a. True
b. False

11. If you grumble when things go wrong you will gloat when they prosper
a. True
b. False

12. God can take each and every natural event and use it for our training.
a. True
b. False

13. No good thing dwells in me
a. True
b. False

14. God can take the experience of serving under a poor tutor to train us
a. True
b. False

15. A good steward is more concerned with the bigger things
a. True
b. False

Chapter 18

THE FLOW OF GOD'S SPIRIT

Being Naturally Spiritual and Spiritually Natural

WHEN THE SPIRITUAL life of God was separated from Adam there remained an empty hole in him. How he longed for those evenings in the garden walking and talking with God. When serious family issues like murder and every other kind of sin rose up where could Adam turn? He was separated. Death's toll began to take effect. Gradually mankind sank into every kind of horrible sin and injustice against one another.

Jesus came to bring man back into right relationship with the Father. He sent His Spirit to dwell IN us. Again we have the opportunity to walk with the Father and talk with Him through His Spirit in us. The way has been restored. Praise the Lord!

Jesus prayed for us that we would be in Him and He in us so that we could be ONE. The same heart, the same plan, the same Spirit.

It should be natural for us to be spiritual. That is what

we were created for. That is what the serpent stole and that is what Jesus restored.

Adam did more in a day than walk and talk with God, he was told to subdue and rule over the whole earth. He was to be Spiritually Natural. This means Adam brought the Spirit into everything he did. He talked with God about each and every thing that needed to be done and discussed how best to do it.

Do Not Separate (Compartmentalize) the Spiritual and the Natural

In our lives this is an area where we need to take a close look. Have we separated the natural things from the spiritual? Or do you naturally live your life being where He wants you to be when He wants you to be there doing what He wants you to do? Is it natural for you to feel His compassion for someone and begin to minister to them anywhere anytime? Do you naturally ask Him about everyday things or lean on your own understanding?

It All Flows Together, There is No Separation

Some of us have run our lives like a pie chart. 25% for this and 32% for that. If we let Him have full place in us He will bring the balance we seek.

Let Him into all you do until He is Lord of all and All In ALL. Let Him lead and you follow. This is not difficult. Well, maybe at first; but after all it is how we were made. Learn to enter into THE FLOW OF HIS SPIRIT

The Flow of His Spirit

Depending on His Strength

Load a container for Nigeria, minister deliverance until 2am, up early to cook breakfast for 70, clean out the refrigerators ready for the donations coming in at 10am, get a few guest rooms clean and fresh and don't forget to leave some snacks and water, OK off to minister at the reservation.. getting back at 2am etc, etc, etc. This is how we lived, totally dependent on His strength, guidance and anointing. No, we never burned out; we just burned brighter because we were in the flow of His Spirit where there is perfect rest in doing His Will.

John 4:32 But he said unto them, I have meat to eat that ye know not of.

John 4:34 Jesus said unto them, My meat is to do the will of him that sent me, and to finish his work.

John 6:27 Labor not for the meat which perishes, but for that meat which endures unto everlasting life, which the Son of man shall give unto you: for him hath God the Father sealed.

Leaning on His Wisdom

There is such a process God had to do in all of our lives to bring us from depending on our own understanding to leaning on His Wisdom. It takes trust and it takes training, but if you know He has provided it, that His wisdom is available, you can ask Him for it and press into it. We can cooperate with the Holy Spirit as He brings us into the flow of Gods Spirit of Wisdom.

Situations in people's lives all around us are far too complex to even understand never mind solve, but God can give an answer to a man that will amaze you. Let us learn to receive His wisdom in every situation. He knows all things and wants to tell us things we know not of. He can give us ways to do difficult things that will make them so much easier. He is also concerned about the natural things.

Ephesians 3:5 Which in other ages was not made known unto the sons of men, as it is now revealed unto his holy apostles and prophets by the Spirit; gentleness, boldness, dependence and grace of His Nature and His Character which has been formed in us.

We should not try to do His work in our old carnal ways. We want to learn His Heart and His Nature. God told the Old Testament priests that they were to never put anointing oil on flesh nor try to imitate or duplicate that anointing because it was Holy.

Exodus 30:32 Upon man's flesh shall it not be poured, neither shall ye make any other like it,… it is holy and it shall be holy unto you.

Moving When He is Moving, Rest When He Rests

It was not all work; we loved to fellowship with the Lord and with each other, we loved to take a day and visit a family in need or sit around and talk. We never figured this on a pie chart or studied it in a book; it was orchestrated by His Spirit.

God's people in the desert, having just left Egypt, knew little about the desert life after having lived in Goshen for so many generations. But God knew and He sent a cloud to cover them in the day and a pillar of fire for the night. This was protection from the sun in the day and put Godly fear in their enemies at night. Even snakes don't like fire. His glory was a shield for them so, "the sun would not smite them by day nor the moon by night" (Psalm 121:6) How we need more of His Glory!

Exodus 13:21 And the LORD went before them by day in a pillar of a cloud, to lead them the way; and by night in a pillar of fire, to give them light; to go by day and night: (Exod 40:38; Num 14:14; Deut 1:33; Neh 9:12; Neh 9:19; Ps 78:14; Ps 105:39; 1Cor 10:1)

Ezekiel's Wheel

Ezekiel's description of what he saw has been given many explanations or has just been ignored by some. The living creatures are the four "faces" of Jesus as depicted in the four gospels. The Son of Man, The Kingly Lion of the Tribe of Judah, The Servant of the Most High (the ox), and the Eagle, which is The Son of God. Also found in Rev. 4:7 around the throne of God.

Ezekiel 1:4 And I looked, and, behold, a whirlwind came out of the north, a great cloud, and a fire infolding itself, and a brightness was about it, and out of the midst thereof as the colour of amber, out of the midst of the fire. **5** Also out of the midst thereof came the likeness of four living creatures. And this was their appearance; they had the likeness of a man. **6** And every one had four faces, and every one had four wings. (Ezek. 10:14) **7** And their feet were straight feet; and the sole of their feet was like the sole of a calf's foot: and they sparkled like the color of burnished brass. **8** And they had the hands of a man under their wings on their four sides; and they four had their faces and their wings. (Ezek. 10:8) **9** Their wings were joined one to another; they turned not when they went; they went every one straight forward. **10** As for the likeness of their faces, they four had the face of a man, and the face of a lion, on the right side: and they four had the face of an ox on the left side; they four also had the face of an eagle. **11** Thus were their faces: and their wings were stretched upward; two wings of every one were joined one to another, and two covered their bodies. Ezek 10:14; Rev 4:7

If we focus on more than just the creatures themselves we see how they were moved by the Spirit. Wherever He moved, they moved. And when they moved they went like a flash of lightning straight forward. They did not turn this way or that. We also see God the Father full of glory upon His throne, sending and directing. Whatever the Father did, the Spirit did also. Whatever the Spirit did, Jesus through His people did also. This is the meaning of the wheels. We are the vehicle that He is working through in this world today. We need to be connected one to another by "like spokes on the wheel". God is going to work through a united, networked and "joined at the heart" body of people by the Spirit of the Lord. This is an amazing picture of How God wants to move by His Spirit through His people at the end of time. Let us press in to enter into "Ezekiel's Wheel"

Ezekiel 1:12 And they went every one straight forward: whither the spirit was to go, they went; and they turned not when they went. 13 As for the likeness of the living creatures, their appearance was like burning coals of fire, and like the appearance of lamps: it went up and down among the living creatures; and the fire was bright, and out of the fire went forth lightning. 14 And the living creatures ran and returned as the appearance of a flash of lightning. 19 And when the living creatures went, the wheels went by them: and when the living creatures were lifted up from the earth, the wheels were lifted up. Ezek 10:16 20 Whithersoever the spirit was to go, they went, thither was their spirit to go; and the wheels were lifted up over against them: for the spirit of the living creature was in the wheels. 21 When those went, these went; and when those stood, these stood; and when those were lifted up from the earth, the wheels were lifted up over against them: for the spirit of the living creature was in the wheels.

NOTE: To read more about Ezekiel's Wheel see the Training Pacs transcribed from Rev Agnes Numer's messages. "Ezekiel 1, 2 & 3"

Jesus stood up on the feast Sabbath and declared that out of our bellies would flow rivers of living water and he was speaking of the Holy Spirit. (John 7:38) A river is refreshing, life-giving, thirst-quenching and restful. We can have this river if we will learn to enter into the flow of God's Spirit. This river is referred to many times in the Word of God but an especially powerful picture is found in Ezekiel 37.

Ezekiel 47:7 Now when I had returned, behold, at the bank of the river were very many trees on the one side and on the other. (Rev. 22:2) 8 Then said he unto me, These waters issue out toward the east country, and go down into the desert, and go into the sea: which being brought forth into the sea, the waters shall be healed.

The River is For the Seas to be Healed

This River that flows out of us is not there just to make us feel good, although there is nothing to compare with His life flowing out of us; its first purpose is to flow out into the seas (of humanity) and bring healing. It flows out from the throne of God into the thirsty desert. Our calling and our purpose is to pour out His life into the sea of people who are so thirsty for Jesus. When they truly see Him reflected in us they will come to Him. He said, "And I, if I be lifted up will draw all men unto me". But will we allow Him to remove the junk out of our lives and train us to enter into this great FLOW OF HIS SPIRIT into the desert?

REVIEW: THE FLOW OF GOD'S SPIRIT

1. God is more concerned with spiritual things than natural
a. True
b. False

2. It should be natural for us to be spiritual
a. True
b. False

3. It is all right for us to separate the spiritual and natural in our lives
a. True
b. False

4. We can bring the Spirit into everything we do
a. True
b. False

5. We were created to let Him lead and we would follow
a. True

b. False

6. It is natural for God's people to hear His voice
a. True
b. False

7. We should be careful not to burn out while flowing by His Spirit
a. True
b. False

8. To beautifully Flow by His Spirit we have to learn:
a. How to paddle upstream
b. How to become more motivated
c. Not to lean on our own wisdom
d. How to depend on other people

9. When we know His will we should always wait for Him to move us
a. True
b. False

10. Once we know it's God's will we just need to aggressively get it done
a. True
b. False

11. Ezekiel's Wheel is an amazing picture of How God wants to move by His Spirit through His people at the end of time
a. True
b. False

12. When Jesus declared that out of our bellies would flow rivers of living water, he was speaking of the Holy Spirit.
a. True
b. False

13. This River that flows out of us is there to make us feel good
a. True
b. False

14. Our calling and our purpose is to pour out His life into the sea of people who are so thirsty for Jesus
a. True
b. False

15. When people truly see Christ reflected in us they will come to Him
a. True
b. False

Chapter 19
MINISTERING BY THE SPIRIT OF THE LORD

How the Training Began

WHEN GOD SPOKE to Agnes in 1954 as she was washing her dishes on a Sunday He told her, "Go into your living room and read Isaiah 58." Agnes relates the incident, ". . . So as I dried my hands and walked out of my kitchen into my living room, the Spirit of the Lord came like a mighty covering big as the outdoors. All at once I began to feel that something was beginning to happen to me." As she began to read, the Lord showed her semi-trucks and planes and warehouses and food. There were centers here and there around the world where people could go and receive spiritually and naturally. We later called them training centers. They can also be called "Goshens" or "Cities of refuge".

One day, in 1967, God spoke to Agnes again and said, "The vision no longer tarries, it is here" He told her, "It is time to start the training". So she began to make plans to set up trailers, to make classrooms and the Lord told her, "I said that I was going to do it." So Agnes said, "Then I am going to let You do it." So the training began right there in her living room in Littlerock, California. And God sent the people, a few at first, but then people came from all around the world. And God would minister to them and they would receive a vision and then go and run with it.

Agnes never claimed to be a preacher or teacher or an apostle. She claimed that God had called her to preach and teach by the Spirit of the Lord. She would only minister when the Spirit of God began to move her. She stayed in that flow of His Spirit for over 50 years.

Teaching/Preaching by the Spirit of the Lord

Impartation into the Spirit, not education of the mind

Although so many ministers are familiar with studying all of the Greek and Hebrew and breaking every phrase down and cross referencing them, what often is produced is "head knowledge". That kind of knowledge can only go from your head to the head of another person. It does not impart God's Word inside of you so that you change as the word is being given.

The Holy Spirit kind of ministering that we received was by impartation where God would take a part of His own revelation knowledge and place it in our spirits. It would then be a part of us. We could then run with it. He did not just tell us where we fell short and how we ought to be, He gave into our spirits what we ought to be and His word changed us. He imparted His Heart inside of us. He would place a vision within us and we could "see" what He was saying.

There were times as Agnes would Teach by the Spirit of the Lord that she would tell us, "this is as new to me as it is to you". She would be receiving wisdom, knowledge and revelation as the Holy Spirit gave it to her and she would minister it to us. Those were the times we could feel His powerful presence in a special way.

Transformation

When the Word came forth with power to convict us of something the grace of God came with it to change us at the same time. As soon as we admitted our error in our own hearts He was already changing us. The Word of Truth confronted lies that we had believed. Once we accepted and sided with the Truth we were made free. So often this divine exchange transformed us. As the Word "mirrored" our fault and we would confess/agree with the truth there was the grace and power to become what that Word was proclaiming. What a mighty divine exchange would happen night after night. We looked forward to the next meeting to see what God was going to do next. What anticipation. What Glory. What anointing. How precious.

Vision

God loves to reveal His heart and His plans to a people who will hear His voice and "agree" with Him. The Lord sent people to Agnes' house that already had vision and they would share, He sent people with no vision or a cloudy one so they could receive one. God is always doing and speaking. He always has a plan and a vision. He is never confused, hopeless or lost for ideas. He is simply full of creative, nation changing ideas, plans and strategies and He loves to "download" these to us.

We had many spontaneous conferences where God would send many people at the same time from different places without human coordination. He would orchestrate divine connections between them and help people to network together in the work of His Kingdom. We seldom had scheduled appointments for people because He would lead them there at just the right time for His purpose. In fact day after day, non-stop for years, one group would be leaving as the next unannounced group would be coming in. From all around the world God caused them to come. And He let them see what He was doing there, in the spiritual and the natural, and they would go home with a new understanding of God and His plans and His ways. They had seen a little of God's Kingdom come on Earth.

Worship/Intercession/Warfare

That 10 acre, Littlerock California, property was a small, quaint place in the Mojave Desert. There was nothing unusual about what you saw as you drove between the cypress trees up to the main house. Perhaps there were more people around than at most homes, and we had added mobile homes and semi-trucks and trailers and a couple warehouses and a small doublewide school building. Agnes' house was a red and white mission style duplex that had been joined years ago. An archway covered with roses over a quaint sidewalk led up to the house between overhanging tree boughs. But there was something different – a certain lightness in the atmosphere that you could not mistake. It felt like Jesus. It felt like some place Holy. As you came in the house into the living room you were greeted with love and served with grace. Everyone who came was fed and blessed in every way. Everyone was treated as a "special guest". You might hear someone humming in worship as they served, or praying for someone over in another corner. Children were everywhere. You could sense God's Presence abiding there.

But when the meeting would begin it was like nothing you may ever have experienced. That quiet people would sing and dance and praise and rejoice. Sometimes they would storm heaven on behalf of a need far away or in the room. Men, women and children all in one small living room with one purpose; they were hungry to meet with God. Happy and free or Running through troops and leaping over walls like mighty men at war. The awesome presence of God was overpowering to the flesh and the demonic forces. Thousands of people were set free as we experienced more than 40 years of an outpouring of God's Spirit every day of the week.

Simultaneous Praise/Deliverance/Prophesy

When God began to move as we entered into praising Him we would never know when prayer or deliverance would break out. Someone would be moved by God to pray for someone and His anointing would fall on them. Other people would support that person. The leading and anointing often would touch first one and then another. There was no program but there was divine order. Whenever a prophetic word came forth we would sing more quietly and make sure the person heard The Word of the Lord to them. This flowing of God's Spirit might continue for hours.

We all were in training by His Spirit and sometimes we would make mistakes. Those who had more training were used to help those who were learning. We were all learners, He was the trainer, and we had so much joy when we "heard right" and God would use us.

God used the Children

Matthew 19:13 Then little children were brought to him for him to lay his hands on them and pray. But the disciples scolded those who brought them. (Mark 10:13; Luke 18:15) 14 But Jesus said, "Let the little children come to me and do not try to stop them, for the kingdom of heaven belongs to such as these." (Matt 18:3; 1Cor 14:20; 1Pet 2:2) 15 And he placed his hands on them and went on his way.

Beautifully, the Spirit of the Lord would choose one of the children. They sometimes would be able to break through to see someone set free where the adults had not been able. One day a two year old began to cry from her crib and wanted her mother to pick her up. She then walked to where we were praying for a particularly stubborn man. When her mother finally discerned that the child wanted to pray she lifted her to where she could reach the man's head. While putting her two little hands on his head she cried out, "Hear, Hear, Hear". The man fell back and God was able to break that stubborn spirit which had bound him.

When serious prayer needs were phoned in, it was the children who seemed to have a special place in Father God's heart and he would answer when they prayed. Many, many countless miracles happened and many people called for prayer. Children are more natural at flowing by the Spirit of the Lord than many adults. He will teach them if we will allow them to learn.

Daily, extended, unlimited, meetings with God

Lunch would wait; sleep was optional, when God was moving. Agnes was precise about starting at the set time but only God decided the ending time. If the children were sleepy they lay down somewhere and were carried to their beds later. Our greatest desire was to know God and move with Him.

This is central – other priorities yield to this

Even when a container had to be filled or a truck unloaded; if God was moving in that living room we all would be there until He lifted. Then we would tackle the job at hand with vigor. To our surprise our jobs all were accomplished by His help.

Outreach, Evangelism, Children's Church, Funerals, Overseas Missions, Senior Centers, House Meetings, etc.

When God first brought Agnes to that little mission style house with the redwood ceiling and walls He spoke to her and said, "You will not go out or come in unless I send you. I will bring people to your door from every nation and people". He told her that she would impart a vision to them, "that they that run may read it" (Hab. 2:2) And so He did. He brought thousands through that front door to sit next to Agnes or take a tour with her staff so that they that "read it may run with it". We know that what God gave us is a small demonstration of His Kingdom on Earth but we know that it is not for us; it is for the whole world. It is a model for the body of Christ and for the end of time.

At the age of 60 God started taking Agnes to the nations. We have some amazing stories how God used her which time and space will not permit. She travelled to many nations 5 or 6 times and we were sometimes blessed to be included on her teams. God birthed ministries and raised up leaders everywhere He took her. The same pouring forth of the river of God was experience in so many places. There are ministries still thriving in many of those places until today. Agnes has given the word of the Lord to Generals in Israel, leaders in Africa, church fathers in Asia and even the Pope but she always noticed and loved the common people in their need and often it was these whom God raised up to be mighty leaders.

One humble family that Agnes prophesied to in India in a small house in the ghetto now has a ministry directed by the son with orphanages, and churches and a new house in a good area just like she spoke it. When we visited them recently those churches are doing well and the orphanage is beautiful, but most of all, the same beautiful Love of God and flow of His Spirit is THERE. This was the way God used her and now through so many of us who received the impartation, this is the way God continues to minister through us.

REVIEW: MINISTERING BY THE SPIRIT OF THE LORD

1. Impartation into your spirit changes you as you receive the Word
a. True
b. False

2. Head knowledge can only go from your head and be imparted into another person's spirit
a. True
b. False

3. When God's Spirit is ministering by impartation you receive His heart and His vision
a. True
b. False

4. A Christian can be transformed as he accepts and sides with Truth as it is being ministered
a. True
b. False

5. God loves to download nation changing ideas, plans and strategies to his people
a. True
b. False

6. God's Kingdom work must be carefully scheduled to avoid confusion
a. True
b. False

7. The awesome presence of God is overpowering to the flesh and the demonic forces
a. True
b. False

8. We should be careful to always separate deliverance, praise and prophesy to avoid confusion
a. True
b. False

9. It is possible to have order without a program, a specific leader or an agenda
a. True
b. False

10. Children can be more natural at flowing by the Spirit of the Lord than many adults
a. True
b. False

Chapter 20

CHRIST IN YOU THE HOPE OF GLORY

The Revelation of Jesus to Us

THROUGHOUT HISTORY JESUS has revealed Himself to His people, and when He did their lives were never the same. Once you meet Him it changes you. There are no words to adequately describe our experiences with Him. Often He does not reveal Himself all at once in one grand experience. Those glimpses of Him that we carry in our hearts, if added together, begin to form a "full revelation" of Jesus Christ. We see Him afresh in the Word, or someone is ministering and we get another glimpse. In our quiet times, or going through the day He shows up and we "see" Him more clearly. The more we see Him the more we become like Him.

1John 3:2 Beloved, now are we the sons of God, and it doth not yet appear what we shall be: but we know that, when he shall appear, we shall be like him; for we shall see him as he is.

Let's read Isaiah 6.

God came and Isaiah saw the Lord, He was seated on a throne.

He heard, "Holy, Holy, Holy, The Commander of Armies, His Majesty and splendor fill all the earth".

Isaiah 6:1 In the year of King Uzziah's death, I saw the sovereign master seated on a high, elevated throne. The hem of his robe filled the temple. (2Kgs 15:7) **2** Seraphs stood over him; each one had six wings. With two wings they covered their faces, with two they covered their feet, and they used the remaining two to fly. (Rev 4:8) **3** They called out to one another, "Holy, holy, holy is the Lord who commands armies! His majestic splendor fills the entire earth!" **4** The sound of their voices shook the door frames, and the temple was filled with smoke. **5** I said, "Too bad for me! I am destroyed, for my lips are contaminated by sin, and I live among people whose lips are contaminated by sin. My eyes have seen the king, the LORD who commands armies." **6** But then one of the seraphs flew toward me. In his hand was a hot coal he had taken from the altar with tongs. 7 He touched my mouth with it and said, "Look, this coal has touched your lips. Your evil is removed; your sin is forgiven." (Jer 1:9, Dan 10:16) **8** I heard the voice of the sovereign master say, "Whom will I send? Who will go on our behalf?" I answered, "Here I am, send me!" (NET)

Then Isaiah knew he was unclean and cried out, "This is the end of me", or "No hope for me", because "I and my people are full of sin". We can walk along through our lives as pretty good people in our own eyes until we meet the Lord of Hosts, the one who commands all of the armies of heaven and orchestrates them upon the earth. It is the best place to be when we see our own "undone-ness" and we cry out, "Alas!" When we realize HE is on the throne and not us so many things change.

We do not realize how earnestly our Father God longs to "visit" our evil and remove it and to forgive our sins. (Isaiah 26:12-15) He desires to send that fiery coal from His Holy altar to cleanse us. When we see Him as a Holy, Awesome, Majestic, Commander of heavens mighty hosts we too will have Godly fear and see our sinfulness and repent and be cleansed.

Then God called Isaiah and he responded, "Here am I send me". And God did send and commission Isaiah. And He filled his spirit with the word of the Lord for that people.

John the Baptist:

First, before John the Baptist preached; even though he was called and filled with the Holy Spirit from his mother's womb and even though the prophets had written of him, even though his father was a priest and Jesus was his cousin; the word of the Lord had to come to him before he could preach.

Luke 3:2 Annas and Caiaphas being the high priests, **the word of God came unto John** the son of Zacharias in the wilderness. 3 And he came into all the country about Jordan, preaching the baptism of repentance for the remission of sins;

Ezekiel:

In the first three chapters in this book, Jesus reveals Himself to Ezekiel, then he Calls Ezekiel and then He trains Ezekiel, putting His words in Ezekiel's' mouth. He taught him how to work with a stubborn and obstinate people. God gave him a forehead of adamant so he would not be affected by the people; he would just give them the Word of the Lord. We too need to be "delivered from the people" (Acts 26:17, Jer. 15:20)

Ezekiel 3:9 As an adamant harder than flint have I made thy forehead: fear them not, neither be dismayed at their looks, though they [be] a rebellious house.

Paul: "That I might minister"

Similar to us today, Paul never met Jesus personally, "in the flesh". but He did meet him on the road to Damascus and it changed his whole life. (Acts 9:1-9) After that he also received a revelation in which Jesus gave him the gospel he was called to preach to the gentiles. Then he spent 11 years in the desert of Arabia being trained by the Holy Spirit.

Galatians 1:11 Now I want you to know, brothers and sisters, that the gospel I preached is not of human origin. **12** For I did not receive it or learn it from any human source; instead **I received it by a revelation of Jesus Christ**. **13** For you have heard of my former way of life in Judaism, how I was savagely persecuting the church of God and trying to destroy it. **14** I was advancing in Judaism beyond many of my contemporaries in my nation, and was extremely zealous for the traditions of my ancestors. **15** But when the one who set me apart from birth and called me by his grace was **pleased 16 to reveal his Son IN ME so that I could preach** him among the Gentiles, I did not go to ask advice from any human being, 17 nor did I go up to Jerusalem to see those who were apostles before me, but right away I departed to Arabia, and then returned to Damascus.

Above his Damascus experience, the revelation he received from Jesus and the Baptism of the Holy Spirit there was a time in Paul's life that he began to discover Jesus Christ IN HIM, flowing out of him, anointing him, moving through him. This is what enabled and qualified him to preach.

Perhaps the first apostles could have argued that he was not qualified; after all they had spent over 3 years with Jesus and Paul hadn't. Paul's past life was very tainted; in fact he had directed the movement to exterminate them all.

WHAT QUALIFIED PAUL IS THE SAME THING WE NEED TODAY:
God had chosen Saul.
Jesus revealed himself to Saul.
Jesus brought revelation of the gospel to him and sent him to the Gentiles.
Then Jesus began to reveal Himself within Paul so that he could preach
When this happens you know "it is no longer I, but Christ who lives in me". (Gal 2:20) Paul did not immediately go to the apostles in Jerusalem and seek their approval; he just began to allow Jesus to minister through him. He began to do what Jesus in him was doing. Jesus was taking him to the Gentiles and so he went.

Christ in You the Hope of Glory

Colossians 1:27 God wanted to make known to them the glorious riches of this mystery among the Gentiles, which is Christ in you, the hope of glory. 28 We proclaim him by instructing and teaching all people with all wisdom so that we may present every person mature in Christ. 29 Toward this goal I also labor, struggling according to his power that powerfully works in me.

To the Gentiles Paul was a perfect example how the "greatest of all sinners" and the "least of all saints" could experience living in glorious freedom from sin and the old nature. Just as Paul had been changed they could be changed through experiencing **Christ living within them**. He instructed, taught and imparted wisdom to them all until they became **mature in Christ**. This clearly was Paul's goal for each of the churches where he ministered.

Ephesians 4:11 It was he who gave some as apostles, some as prophets, some as evangelists, and some as pastors and teachers, **12** to equip the saints for the work of ministry, that is, to build up the body of Christ, **13 until we all attain** to the unity of the faith and of the knowledge of the Son of God – a mature person, attaining to the measure of Christ's full stature. (NET)

The prophets, evangelists, apostles, pastors, teachers were only the means to **the goal** which was building up the body of Christ until we all know HIM and until we all are developed into the fullness of the Stature of Christ; **so that we all "might minister"**.

Fullness of the Stature of Christ Ministry

We can only minister what we are. We can only witness what we have seen. How we need Jesus to reveal Himself to us. How we need to be: called by Him, trained by Him, equipped by Him, empowered by Him, and sent by Him and how desperately the world needs us to **minister by His Spirit**.

If we cannot see this mark we will never shoot for it. If we have never seen this "mystery" we cannot press into it. If we do not have people like Paul in our lives, who instruct, teach and correct us how will we know? "We can know as we follow on to know the Lord". (Hosea 6:3) He will Train us by His Spirit, He will form the very image of His Son in us, He will pour His word into us, He will give us the forehead of adamant if we need it, He will send us and He will take us; but we have to know and believe that this is possible. We have to know that God has a "high calling of God in Christ Jesus" for us to enter into. (Philippians 3:14, Hebrew 3:1)

It is our enemies' purpose to keep us from seeing, believing and receiving. Our flesh prefers not to go through the "process" and the training; so it is easier to "remain carnal", but for those who desire it, there is a **ministry by His Spirit**. For lack of better words, let us call this the "Fullness of Stature Ministry" This is where Christ has been born in us and formed in us and He is coming forth in us. It is where He is ministering through us. When we have a mature stature of Christ in us He will minister in power through us.

This is not just a "high sounding" teaching to "tickle the ears". It is straight from the word of God, and we have seen it in reality through the life of Agnes Numer and those whom God raised up through her ministry.

Once He has been able to accomplish a larger degree of processing in our lives, the self-ambition and pride will have given way to the true Love of Christ. We cannot be moved with His compassion and our ambition at the same time. He will deal with all that is not of Him if we eagerly seek Him and cooperate with Him. He will not do it without us and we cannot do it without Him.

Our Only Hope of Glory

Without Him, all of our best efforts are vain. Our only hope of attaining to the glory of God flowing through us is Christ IN Us, The Hope of Glory. The only hope we have of ministering Jesus to others and seeing them grow up into a maturity is **Christ Ministering THROUGH Us in His Glory**. He wants to flow through us like rivers flowing out into the desert to bring healing to the nations. Amen.

REVIEW: CHRIST IN YOU, THE HOPE OF GLORY

1. God often reveals himself to us in one grand experience
a. True
b. False

2. The more we see Him the more we become like Him
a. True
b. False

3. Which answer best describes the phrase, "I am undone"? (Is. 6:5 KJV)
a. There is no hope for me
b. My lips are contaminated by sin
c. This could be the end of me
d. All of the above

4. In which scripture do we learn that God wants to visit our evil and remove it
a. John 10:12
b. Isaiah 26:12-15
c. Jeremiah 30:10

d. Luke 3:2:7

5. John The Baptist's priestly heritage and the ancient prophesies about him qualified him to preach
a. True
b. False

6. God gave Ezekiel a forehead of adamant so:
a. He could break rock to build a road
b. He would not be affected by the stubborn people
c. He would not love the people where God was sending him
d. He could better understand the people

7. What qualified Paul to preach was that:
a. He was born of a priestly line and was highly educated in the scriptures
b. He had spent 3 years with Jesus as a disciple
c. he began to experience Jesus Christ IN HIM, flowing out of him, anointing him to minister
d. He was approved by the other apostles in Jerusalem

8. What was Paul's goal for the Gentiles he preached to?
a. That they would become the largest churches in Asia
b. That they would come to know the scriptures as he ministered
c. That they would become mature in Christ
d. That they could have a revelation of the mystery he preached about

9. The goal was to establish Apostles, Pastors, Prophets, Teachers and evangelists in each place

a. True
b. False

10. Our only hope of attaining to the glory of God flowing through us is:
a. Attending the best seminary
b. Christ in Us, the hope of Glory
c. Being ordained as an apostle
d. Memorizing whole chapters in preparation for preaching

Chapter 21
GOD'S LOVE DEMONSTRATED

Jehovah Jireh – God provides everything

WHAT A WONDERFUL JOY we have had for over 50 years. We have lacked nothing. He has been our Jehovah Jireh. Please understand, this means we did not need to go to the store, we did not have fundraisers, and we did not send out letters of solicitation or have a "partner list", or a grant. People would just give as the Lord moved on their heart. If we ever asked for anything it was not for our own selves, it was for the poor or for the nations. We had plenty; plenty to give and plenty besides. Every person gave of themselves freely, voluntarily, no one received a salary, and God was the provider.

He delights in caring for His people. Some examples:

- Israel – no lack in the desert.
- Jesus – birds/foxes – nowhere to lay his head.

- Paul – abound/be in want – the gift of being content.
- Elijah – fed in time of famine – ravens, widow and an angel.
- Isaac – blessed in famine, given 100 fold harvest in drought. (Genesis 25, 26)
- Early Church – Sold/shared what they had, heavy persecution. Later provided by money collected by the concerned Gentile churches.

Yes, there were many occasions, just like Jesus and the seven loaves and two fish, where God multiplied the food. There was always enough to give to all who came. We did not send people away empty; usually the biggest problem was that the needy person's car was not large enough to fit all of the blessings.

Joel 2:26 And ye shall eat in plenty, and be satisfied, and praise the name of the LORD your God, that hath dealt wondrously with you: and my people shall never be ashamed.

No, this does not only work in America. All of our sister ministries in every part of the world have learned to LOOK TO HIM for their every need. In fact it is as we pour out of "our **own** bread to feed the hungry" that we are filled. How do you feed 200 orphans in India when most families cannot even feed themselves? Jehovah Jireh! How do you have a food distribution in America that feeds 15,000 people a week? Jehovah Jireh! How can you help 85 widows celebrate Christmas in Nigeria? Of course, Only Jehovah Jireh! Tents, food and medicine in Northern Pakistan? No problem for Jehovah Jireh!

Yes, we know Him as Jehovah Jireh, and you can too. When you see the need and begin to give "whatever is in your hand" then He will provide more than enough. For His Name is JEHOVAH JIREH. He is more than enough, the all sufficient one, God Almighty.

Demonstrating God's Love to the Poor

Food Distribution

First, came the vision and then the provision. The provision began small and grew as our capacity to believe and receive increased. Soon we needed a pickup truck, then a bobtail truck, then a semi to carry it all.

On the more practical side, distributing food to the needy is a balance of how much food is available, how much can you receive (logistics, trucks, fuel, hours, drivers etc.), how many people are you giving to, how many volunteers are willing to help and how much does it cost to do it. We have seen God keep this all in balance for us for all of these years. We totally depend on Him and give Him the glory.

We love to give God's provision; whether to a small family or thousands of people, we can always feel the Love of God being demonstrated to the people. We always tell them, "This is God's provision for you. You thank him for this blessing. We did not buy it; He provided it because He loves you."

Meals and Hospitality

In every culture for many generations hospitality is how love was expressed to both friends and strangers. In God's culture, He loves to serve people and welcome them. One of the final events coming up at the end of time is a huge wedding feast. God taught his people to have both lavish feasts as well as fasts. He built magnificent celebrations into the culture of His people. Jesus spent many intimate moments with people over a meal. He was accused of being a glutton by some of the religious crowd. Jesus loves people.

Every guest who came was offered drinks and asked if they had eaten. "You must stay for lunch or snack or something." And the meals that came out of that little kitchen, WOW! God's provision with His loving wisdom made some of the most amazing meals. A lot of care went into them because we were serving the people of God. We were doing it unto Him.

In the culture we had, living together with 60 or 80 people, there was always a birthday party, anniversary or something grand to celebrate. Some of our "meetings" began or ended with cake and ice cream, coffee or tea. We did love to make every birthday an occasion for that special person. How many people would weep because of the love they felt, often for the first time in their life! The natural and the spiritual just flowing together in a beautiful, exuberant, family way.

The Widow, the Orphan and the Transient

Besides our central scripture in Isaiah 58, the poor and needy are referred to everywhere in the Bible. The word "poor" is used 200 times. "Need and Needy" 162 times. "Destitute and Oppressed" 48 times. "widow" 82, "orphan or fatherless" 44 etc.

There are many promises linked to caring for the people just mentioned. Our lives begin to take on new meaning when God pours through our vessels to touch the most vulnerable in our world through His love.

Psalm 72, written by King David to His son Solomon, blesses his son to be a good king and describes what a "good" kingdom would look like. The Kingdom of God demonstrated on earth with King Jesus on the throne would look like everything written in this Psalm and more. A community of people with Jesus on the throne would also be taking care of the poor and the needy. Please read for yourselves and be blessed.

Serving the needy was a practice of the early church. They often ate together and always remembered the needy. That's where Steven developed his ministry, serving tables. Paul made it his concern as he traveled, to make collections for the poor. Certainly, carrying that much money was a risky ministry. The church in Jerusalem was supported this way when the persecution was so heavy that they could not have jobs and their funds from selling their homes and properties were running low.

Job, in claiming his integrity, said he had cared for the widow, the fatherless, the orphan and the sojourner. (Job 31:15 – 21)

The temple in the Old Testament was the place God designated to gather provisions for the poor, the widow and the transient. It was originally, the way God desired things, that it would be the responsibility of the church to care for these people; it was not the government's duty. It is only in recent times that social welfare and government programs were instituted.

Disaster Relief

God has clearly promised that at the end of time there will be an increase of wars, calamities and natural and spiritual disasters. He who promised blessings also promised persecution. When Crisis comes to the lives of a people they are the most open to spiritual things. God makes the most sense to someone when they have no answer in themselves, the government has no answer and something has just "shaken everything that can be shaken" in their life. We should be ready to "give an answer" to these people in very practical ways.

Intercession: How many times disasters were diverted through intense, Holy Spirit breathed intercession will only be known by God Himself. Only He knows what the hours of travail were for. He only sees the results. There are times, however, that we knew more specifically what we were praying for as he gave understanding. Those experiences in prayer were very profound as we all would gather in the living room and call upon the Living God to intervene in world affairs. We also were lead to repent on behalf of God's people as Daniel and Ezra did to avert God's hand of Judgment and release His Mercy (Daniel 9 and Ezra 9)

Preparation: Training, Supplies, Practice, Networking and Experience.

The Holy Spirit will give wisdom to all who will listen. The wise man will hear and obey and be prepared. (Matthew 7:24-25) Building on the Rock is having a lifestyle based on Wisdom from God. We need an ear to hear the Lord say, "Ye must be prepared to demonstrate my Love in the midst of Disaster".

Receiving semi-trucks and distributing food to 15,000 people a week is great disaster response training in itself. We feel it also has helped to train God's people in our valley who have been our distributors. Conducting large community outreach events also has helped train us and others.

Loving the desperate and needy takes a special grace which is learned with practice as we call upon Him for more love as we meet the unlovely. The relationships and the network that is formed through weekly distribution and community events is key to responding to local crises. When needy people come to churches regularly they develop a trust and that church will naturally become a distribution center in times of major crisis.

Supplies that will keep long term are stored for the future and rotated to keep a stock on hand "just in case". Networking relationships with large disaster response organizations help to prepare and make disaster plans.

Response:

- **Immediate**. Our people have been in the middle of some of the worlds famed crises; Mount Pinatubo, When Communism fell in Russia, Katrina, Orissa's super cyclone, Northern Pakistan earthquake, etc. Somehow God knows how to place His people in the best place to bring Him glory.
- **Long Term**. Most of our work has been in the Rebuilding phase. Sending supplies and teams to help rebuild and minister is so meaningful to people. They will know we are His children by our Love. It is not the work we do but the Spirit flowing through us while we work. It is who He is within us that shines out and touches them.

Unity: If we will apply ourselves to developing relationships now that align us in unity; when a Crisis comes, we can work together to Respond and Rebuild. Those who have separated themselves now may have no one to call to when they are in need. Much of our work presently is based on years of investment in our own valley by Agnes Numer, we are working where she gained favor and formed relationships that are helping to unify God's people to be ready and to make plans to work together in that "Big Day".

Daily Crises: There are mini disasters in family's lives all around us on a daily basis. If we are ready for a major crisis, we will be much better prepared to respond to those who frequently find themselves in need around us. May we have eyes to see and ears to hear the cries of the brokenhearted and respond by His Love!

Rehabilitation/Discipleship

The enemy has set many traps for our flesh to fall into. One of the most difficult to extract ourselves from is drug, alcohol or sexual addiction. An individual in this trap will seldom remain free without the support of a tough love, spiritual, family who understand accountability and know how to work together with the Lord to fight for that freedom.

We have seen hundreds come and seen God deliver them from these snares. They found new meaning and purpose in "giving back" to the community. Our ministry with Isaiah 58 at the core has provided real life training; socially, physically, mental, and spiritually 24 hours a day. These people were able to reenter society with a training they never had as a child. God visited the "Other Lords" who had rule over them, He healed their broken heart and gave them a vision for their future and a hope to be a blessing in life. The Word had to become flesh within them and set them free.

Appropriate technology

Why are we talking about "Community Development"? It is because of the Love of God. Because of Isaiah 58 which commands us to "build up the old waste places". It is God's love DEMONSTRATED through us to a people in need; bringing God's Will on earth. Sending containers is sometimes necessary but Holy Spirit directed, sustainable, community development is by far the most effective means of obliterating Satan's resistance to the gospel which has been built up in a community.

Opportunity is an incredibly powerful term that simply means "to give a person a chance to succeed, prosper, be blessed or survive". Many bondages are broken when a people have hope and **opportunity**. An idea that works, a technology which will succeed, a method which will save labor or cost and a plan which is do-able, all provide **Opportunity** for an individual and a community who were hopeless.

The word "appropriate" means to be suitable to the situation. We are looking at technology which meets the need of a people while being considerate of their environment, their ethics, their culture and their social, political and economic structures. An appropriate technology project must use materials locally available and affordable without harming their environment or undermining their culture. A great idea in one culture would fail in another.

Sustainability means that whatever you have done will continue long after you are gone. The best projects become part of the fabric of the society. They believe it was their idea and so it lifts the standard of living for generations to come. In some societies it would be best done by the women, in others the men. Sometimes we must go to the youth and tap into their forward thinking tendencies. How we must work with each people requires us to have sensitivity to the Spirit of God and to the people. It is God who desires to "TAKE" us to the nations and demonstrate through us WHO HE IS. He knows what will shift the spiritual direction of a nation and He will train us and guide us in the way to approach each community.

Many people ask, "If God was really a God of love, why is there so much suffering in the world?"

Part of this answer is, "because today in the world God is working through His Church and so many of His people are too busy inside the four walls of their church building to consider being His hands extended to the ones He loves so much who are outside, hungry, needy, homeless and destitute. It is because the church has lost its direction of "going into all the world". It is because we have made a business of religion instead of being available to God as His Love manifest to those He died for."

A demonstration of the Kingdom of God on earth: What would it look like?

Kings and farmers alike came to see King David's palatial estates. Even the poor of the land were rich men. Gold and silver littered the streets. Wisdom and Grace prevailed everywhere. This was what it looked like with God directing the king to lead His people.

People had time to write great music, for art and build amazing architecture. This was a Kingdom of People blessed by God. These were God's chosen people living in obedience to Him.

The way we have lived at All Nations International and Sommer Haven has drawn thousands of God's people for over 50 years to see the "model" and receive an impartation of the vision and heart of God the Father. They see the provision, they feel His love, and they see the unity. He is the King and we are His people. This is the Father's Heart. This is what He desires. To show how beautiful He is through a people who will lay down their lives to follow Him. We live by His principles, seek His wisdom and worship Him. What you see in the natural, is how He "Demonstrates His love for us" and through us to our community and to our world. Many who come leave with a new understanding of God's vision for His people and for His world and they "begin to build" according to that vision.

It is His Love, His Provision and His Glory

There is nothing good that has been done which we have done ourselves. It is His Love which is in us. It is His Provision that has been poured out through us. It is He that should receive all of the Praise, Honor and Glory.

REVIEW: GOD'S LOVE DEMONSTRATED

1. Which answer is not an example of God's provision
a. Elijah – fed in time of famine
b. Isaac – blessed in famine
c. Hezekiah – the gift of being content
d. Israel – no lack in the desert

2. God's abundant provision only works in America
a. True
b. False

3. You can know God as Jehovah Jireh by:
a. beginning to give "whatever is in your hand"
b. getting a little red pickup truck
c. getting all the churches together
d. praying until a knock comes to your door

4. With Jehovah Jireh which comes first?
a. Budget
b. Provision
c. Vision

d. A board meeting

5. For many generations love has been expressed by :
a. A hug
b. A smile
c. Greeting cards
d. Hospitality

6. When you serve the people God loves, you are doing it unto Him
a. True
b. False

7. Which Psalm describes what the Kingdom of God would look like under King Jesus
a. Psalm 24
b. Psalm 72
c. Psalm 85
d. Psalm 100

8. God arranged for the government to care for the widows and orphans
a. True
b. False

9. What ways can people be served regarding Crisis which is a time that they are more open to God
a. Intercession
b. Preparation
c. Response
d. All the above

10. How can we apply ourselves now that helps us work together during a crisis
a. Memorizing scripture
b. Developing Relationships
c. Getting Fit by weight training
d. Having plenty of supplies stored up

11. One reason there is so much suffering in this world today is because God is looking for someone to work through.
a. True False

12. God loves to bless and flourish His people
a. True
b. False

13. When we keep what God has given us we eventually will have everything we ever dreamed of
a. True
b. False

14. The Father's heart is to show how beautiful He is through a people who will lay down their lives and follow Him
a. True
b. False

15. God pours His provision out so that we can receive glory
a. True
b. False

Chapter 22

DWELLING TOGETHER IN UNITY

Living Together in Unity

ONE OF THE greatest Holy Spirit training grounds which can occur is when God brings together people from many different cultures, accents, backgrounds, ages and levels of "Christ-likeness" They eat and live together and work together brought together by a common vision and purpose that comes from Him. We were able to live together in unity because of the overshadowing cloud of His Love that saturated Sommer Haven. God had chosen to dwell with us and we had made it our personal choice to allow Him to train us by his Spirit through everything that happened and everyone we met. We guarded that unity carefully because our **blessing** and our **"life for evermore"** depended on it. There were many people who were "not easy to love" and those became our greatest blessing because they offered us the most effective training because we had to rely on His grace, wisdom and understanding to live with them.

"There the Lord Commands a Blessing"

Psalm 133:1 Behold, how good and how pleasant it is for brethren to dwell together in unity! 2 It is like the precious ointment upon the head, that ran down the beard, even Aaron's beard: that went down to the skirts of his garments; 3 As the dew of Hermon, and as the dew that descended upon the mountains of Zion: for there the Lord commanded the blessing, even life for evermore.

In this scripture unity is compared to a fragrance as sweet as the holy anointing oil; it brings a refreshing as fresh as the morning dew; it brings softness to the skin. God commanded the priests to be anointed with oil before coming in and ministering to Him and so we have to maintain unity before coming to God and expecting Him to receive our offering. The dew upon the hills brought fruitfulness to everything which grew there. We can expect God to multiply our fruitfulness in an atmosphere of unity.

Be ye kind one to another, tender hearted, forgiving one another (Ephesians 4:32)

Brotherly kindness; what you do without being asked, just for loves' sake, because you love your brother. When we practice kindness intentionally we are sowing seeds of healing and life. Pour out a little dew into the garden of a brother's heart; when it grows you will enjoy the fruit of it. Even men can be tender with each other when we dare drop our macho image and take up the image of Christ.

Walking in forgiveness.

Choosing to "not keep account when someone does you wrong". This is Jesus love in us. The love chapter says that "Love hardly even notices when someone does it wrong"; Anyone can count your wrongs but only a close brother shows an example of His grace "seventy times seven". We cannot hope to walk in unity without walking in an attitude of continual forgiveness. Not holding on to wrongs done to us. Not allowing the protective wall of "being more careful next time" to grow up between us. Not letting "the sun go down on your wrath" and when something does aggravate we will keep a clean slate that is "new every morning".

Ephesians 4:26 Be ye angry, and sin not: let not the sun go down upon your wrath:

Taking no offense

First, let us be clear. There will be offenses; (Lk 17:1) but are we going to allow God to bring fruit out of those situations?
  Why Are People Offended?
  We may be offended when **we stumble at the word** because we are disobedient. (1Pet 2:8)
  We may be offended when the **light exposes dark areas** in our life. "We are called out of darkness into His marvelous light." The light exposes darkness and this is uncomfortable and we have a choice to make: Hide and cover or Repent and receive mercy. (1Pet 2:9)
  We may be offended when we are **trying to do it ourselves** and are not humbly depending on Jesus' finished work by Faith. When our good works are shown up as filthy rags it hurts our pride. Something rises up inside ourselves and we say, "I thought I was doing so well." or, "who are

they to tell me.....?" When we do everything we do as unto the Lord, depending on His Spirit we will not be easily offended. Rom 8:5-8 makes it clear that the flesh cannot please God and is enmity against Him. And so it would not be surprising that those who are filled with Him would offend those who are striving to please God by their flesh. Example: Saul and David.

We may be offended when we are not recognized, understood or appreciated. For example: The Jews were offended because, after all, "we are the people of God, we are above the Gentiles and we have our 'heritage'." (1Pet 2:10, Is 8:14) When we are not treated 'special' it is difficult for our flesh. But Jesus, the Son of God, "made Himself of no reputation" and Paul tells us to "have that same mind". (Phil 2:7) If we are not "willing to humble ourselves and take on the form of a servant", then our image or our reputation is getting in our way of serving God with a pure heart. Let God "exalt you in due time". (1 Pet 5:6)

NOTE: We can be righteously offended as Jesus was by Peter when "he savored the things of men and not the things of God". (Matt 16:23) May God help us discern when we are rightly offended and when it is just our flesh.

"As Much as Lies Within You"

Romans 12:18 If it be possible, as much as lieth in you, live peaceably with all men.

Paul was very careful to leave no offense so the ministry would not be blamed (2Cor 6:3) and so his conscience would be clear (Acts 24:16) he said, "I exercise myself to have a good conscience" before all men.

There is great wisdom in Ecclesiastes 10:14. It instructs us that, "yielding pacifies great offenses". Can we take the low road when a brother is offended, even if he is offended by Christ in us; can we, with a soft answer, turn away his wrath? Are we willing to "**restore** such a one in a spirit of meekness, considering our own selves lest we also be tempted"? (Galatians 6:1) Are we willing to be "in travail again until Christ be formed" in our brother or sister?

"Speaking the Truth in Love"

Very often it is not **what we say** but **how we say it,** which offends or adds to the offense. Are we "instructing in meekness" (2Timothy 2:25) or are we "Lording it over them"? (Matthew 20:25)

People know when we sincerely love them and are willing to lay down our lives for them that they might have the gospel. (1John 3:16) Are we willing to love not in word only but in deed and in truth? (1John 3:18)

Every people and culture season their food a little differently. Some foods are hard to eat simply because of how they are seasoned. If we care enough about our brother we will desire to "season it" to be palatable for them. We can ask God for the wisdom that is needed to speak to "them that are without" and who lack in some area.

Colossians 4:5 Walk in wisdom toward them that are without, redeeming the time. 6 Let your speech be always with grace, seasoned with salt, that ye may know how ye ought to answer every man.

"Woe unto him through whom they come" (Luke 17:1 and Matthew 18:17)

This is a warning to us. If someone is offended, let us be careful that they are not just offended by our flesh. Seek to be able to lead by example and let God's truth which is demonstrated through us do the offending. Let it be God's presence that convicts. Let us pray that we can restore and encourage our brother/sister again in His ways. Let us seek to have our conscience clear. Let us protect the UNITY of the brethren and the flow of His Spirit because the commanded blessing depends on it.

Not Forming Soul Ties

There is a blessing in having a friend or someone who likes to do the same things we do, but there is a higher kind of relationship that is even more fulfilling. If we have only experienced natural friendships we might not understand that God is leading us to have fellowship with each other by the Spirit of the Lord. Men and women alike have certain ways of relating to other people and many of these ways produce very surface friendships. We all long for meaningful relationships that will satisfy our thirsty souls but too often we are betrayed, misunderstood, taken advantage of or even rejected.

We often open ourselves up to "the wrong people" and make "soul ties" with them which can affect us for years afterward. Many of God's people are finding freedom through praying to break the soul ties they have made throughout their lives. We unwisely make covenants and agreements with people who are not walking in the same direction we are. "How can two walk together except they be agreed?" (Amos 3:3) God made us for fellowship with Him and with one another through Him but we must **both** be walking in "agreement with Him".

Truly living together in Unity requires us to relate to one another by the Spirit of the Lord and not by our own flesh. Fleshly relationships remain in the mental, physical and emotional realms. They are natural, earthly, carnal and human. These relationships involve sympathy instead of compassion; unity of likes, dislikes and ideas instead of unity of purpose, spirit and values; complaining instead of Faith; my need instead of Christ's love demonstrated. When we are united by His Spirit we are first in agreement with Him and then automatically with one another. This is what Jesus prayed to His Father for us; that we may be one with Him and with one another. (John 17:20-23)

Paul purposed in his heart to "know no man after the flesh" but to know the "new creature" and to minister to that "new man" while leading him to be reconciled to God through Christ. (Carefully read 2 Corinthians 5:16-17) Paul's says that his ministry was to see men restored in their relationship to God the Father (ministry of reconciliation).

Agnes often instructed us, "You are here to get to know God, not to make buddies". Carnal relationships lead to more carnality but fellowship leads us to "build up, encourage, provoke (unto good works), be courteous, be kind, serve, and honor each other. (Please read 1 Peter 3:8, 1 Peter 1:22, Hebrews 10:24, 1 Thessalonians 4:9, 1 Thessalonians 3:12, Galatians 5:13, Romans 12:10) So let us aim more at being family who build each other up than at having friends. Dare to confront without compromise, instruct in meekness, love fervently, prefer others as better than yourself, be transparent, honor one another and increase and abound in LOVE one to another. God's LOVE toward each other, even as God has loved us.

Walking in the Light Produces Fellowship

With nothing hidden from God we can walk in His cleansing and renewing power that transforms us from Glory to Glory. When we learn how to quickly admit and confess our faults as the Holy Spirit shines His light on them and **by faith** receive the "cleansing from all unrighteousness" we will walk in the LIGHT. If we do not hold on to offense against our brethren and we walk in forgiveness and love; we are walking in the LIGHT. If we are seeking holy fellowship and not a carnal friendship, we can have communion in the LIGHT.

One of the beautiful things about walking in the light is the **fellowship** we have with God, and another thing is the **unity** we have with those who are also "walking in the light" (John 8:12) with "no part dark" (Luke 11:36) and with the cleansing blood of Jesus actively changing us.

1John 1:7 But if we walk in the light, as he is in the light, we have fellowship one with another, and the blood of Jesus Christ his Son cleanses us from all sin.

When we have been walking in fellowship with each other for a while and we allow a sin in our life or an offense to be in our heart we can feel the difference immediately. Perhaps similar to the longing in God's voice calling out to Adam in the cool of the day, "Adam, where art thou?" This is a unity that can be felt. It builds up and strengthens "as each joint supplies". (Ephesians 4:16) and when that strength and supply is gone we notice.

1 Samuel 23:16 And Jonathan Saul's son arose, and went to David into the wood, and strengthened his hand in God.

Flowing Together

In this hour God desires to have a people who know how to flow together to accomplish His purpose in the Earth. He is looking more to make **a people of God** than a man of God: A people in Unity with Him and one another. Like Joel's army who did not break rank or thrust one another. He said, "This people have I formed for Myself; they shall show forth my praise." (Is 43:21) The Praise and Glory of God in this time will come through a united people. He will demonstrate His Love, His Glory and His Provision through us as we allow Him to prepare us.

Psalm 102:13 Thou shalt arise, and have mercy upon Zion: for the time to favor her, yea, the appointed time, is come. 14 For thy servants take pleasure in her stones, and favor the dust thereof. 15 So the heathen shall fear the name of the LORD and all the kings of the earth thy glory. 16 When the LORD shall build up Zion, he shall appear in his glory. 17 He will regard the prayer of the destitute, and not despise their prayer.

When this was written there was no temple. They longed to build it. All they had were the stones which had laid in ruin, not one on top of the other. But, at least they had the dusty stones. Down through the centuries, each time when the temple was completed, God filled it with His Glory. And with each successive temple, the Glory became greater.

Now God is ready to bring all of His stones (ministries and people) together into a unity under Him as King. It is the appointed time for Him to have compassion on His people. He is ready to form us into a Temple made of "Living Stones" (2 Peter 2:5). When we all come into our places He can do something the world has never seen. He will pour out of His Glory in this new "Temple made without hands" which has been formed by God. We will offer sacrifices that are very acceptable to God and He will respond by pouring forth His Presence. The world is going to see something it has never seen before.

God's Purpose

"When God has built up Zion He will appear in His Glory" (vs16) God is forming this Temple for Him to dwell in for **His own purpose**. It is not just to please us. Verse 17 tells us WHY HE IS DOING IT. It is because, "He has heard the prayer of the destitute and He will not despise their prayer". God desires to have a people, many people and many ministries who will join together with Him in a united purpose of MEETING THE NEEDS OF THE DESTITUTE.

Isaiah 58: 6-8 tells us that He is not pleased with all of our religious activity. God tells us the kind of fasting He wants, He says, "6 Is not the time without eating which I choose, a time to take off the chains of sin, and to take the heavy load of sin off the neck? Is it not a time to let those who suffer under a sinful power go free, and to break every load from their neck? 7 Is it not a time to share your food with the hungry, and bring the poor man into your house who has no home of his own? Is it not a time to give clothes to the person you see who has no clothes, and a time not to hide yourself from your own family? 8 Then your light will break out like the early morning, and you will soon be healed. Your right and good works will go before you. And the shining-greatness of the Lord will keep watch behind you."

The Lord's Splendor in His people comes when we flow together with Him in **demonstrating** His Love, His Provision and His Glory to those who need Him.

REVIEW: DWELLING TOGETHER IN UNITY

1. What blessing does God command over those who dwell together in unity?
a. Financial Increase
b. Anointing and life for evermore
c. Greater provision
d. Being a light in the darkness

2. People who are not easy to love can be our greatest blessing
a. True
b. False

3. In Psalm 133 Scripture likens unity to:
a. Refreshing like the morning dew
b. Dew upon the hills
c. A sweet fragrance
d. All of the above

4. Even men become tender with each other when they take up the image of Christ

a. True
b. False

5. God's word makes it clear that there should never be offenses
a. True
b. False

6. What reason are people offended?
a. When God's word offends us
b. When we are depending on our own ability
c. When we are not noticed and appreciated
d. All of the above

7. It is possible to be righteously offended
a. True
b. False

8. We should be careful not to offend people and keep our conscience clear
a. True
b. False

9. It is not so important how we say something as long as it is the truth
a. True
b. False

10. If we care enough about our brother we will desire to "season it" to be palatable for them
a. True
b. False

11. God's commanded blessing depends on us protecting the unity
a. True
b. False

12. A friendship developed with soul ties will result in deep fellowship
a. True
b. False

13. Fleshly relationships are described as
a. Human, carnal and earthly
b. Based on similar likes and dislikes
c. Based on my needs
d. All of the above

14. Fellowship in relationships leads us to
a. Build up and edify
b. Serve and Honor one another
c. Confront without compromise
d. All of the above

15. When we have been walking in fellowship with someone for a while and one person allows a sin in their life or offense to be in their heart we can feel the difference immediately
a. True
b. False

16. The Lord's Splendor in His people comes when we flow together with Him in demonstrating His Love, His

Provision and His Glory to those who need Him
a. True
b. False

Chapter 23
KINGDOM AUTHORITY

Principles of Kingdom Authority

He Who Is the Greatest Let Him Be the Servant of All

REV. AGNES I. NUMER was a servant to God, ordained by Him, sent by Him, used by Him anointed by Him and provided for by His own hand without fail for over 50 years. He chose her and He spoke through her. He trained her on the back side of the desert for many years; to hear his voice, remove the junk from her life and raise her up as a general in His army.

When he revealed Isaiah 58 to her He said, "This is my plan for my church for the end of time" and "though the vision tarry, wait for it". She had a plan; it was the plan of the Lord. God gave it to her. When no one else was feeding the hungry, she began. When it was still unpopular for the church to teach agriculture, health, micro business, nutrition and various other things, Rev. Agnes I. Numer was traveling the nations and giving them "The Gospel of the Kingdom" in demonstration.

She served the under-served, loved the unlovely, touched the untouchable, and reached the unreachable. God used her to counsel national leaders and paupers alike. She gave them whatever God gave her. When we would go to her for counsel we were not coming to a 'woman', we were coming to the fountain of wisdom and instruction and authority that God poured through her. We knew that God would give her the "words of life" that we needed. (John 6:68)

Agnes ministered by the Spirit of the Lord; by the Spirit of Wisdom, the Spirit of Understanding, the Spirit of Counsel, the Spirit of Might, the Spirit of Knowledge, the Spirit of the Fear of the Lord and the Spirit of the Lord. She did not minister her own wisdom and what she understood, or by her own might. She did not give us her counsel and knowledge. She taught us to fear the Lord and move by His Spirit.

Isaiah 11:2 And the spirit of the LORD shall rest upon him, the spirit of wisdom and understanding, the spirit of counsel and might, the spirit of knowledge and of the fear of the LORD;

Agnes faithfully served to us whatever God placed on her serving platter. It came straight from His kitchen to us and she was His servant joyfully doing His bidding. (Ephesians 6:6)

The Flow of Authority

What gave her the right, ability and power to do these things? Where did she learn this? The right came from God, the power came from Him and so did the ability. Agnes was born just 2 pounds 4 ounces, a premature baby many years before incubators. God gave her life and sustained her. Through the great depression, when many were suffering from hunger, God sustained her. God called her at only 16 years of age and told her that he trained Moses 40 years in Pharaoh's court and 40 more years on the back side of the desert. Agnes answered God, "80 years Lord? If its 80 years, then 80 years it will be!" She died 5 times during her 95 years and God raised her up again and gave her life back because His purpose for her was not finished.

All authority comes from above. It is God given. Judges are ordained by God and must answer to Him. Leaders are subject to Him. Nebuchadnezzar, in possibly the greatest city ever built, had to admit that there is a God in Heaven who RULES OVER ALL and gives authority to whoever He wills.

When the Lord raises someone up He gifts them with His grace and favor. He trains them to follow His Will and they perform His purpose.

Came From Under the Throne of God

There is an authority that flows from out of the throne of God which is found by those who kneel before that throne and hear what He is saying. Those He chooses He empowers. He sends them and they go for Him. This is His Kingdom.

There are so few people who understand the protocol of a king today. Only a few people ever had the opportunity to come near him, and only those who first learned the ways of the palace. Each person who came before the king was instructed in the proper decorum of the kingdom. There was a correct way to address the king and his attendants. For example: If Queen Esther had not been accepted by the scepter she would have died because she came in uninvited. Or another example: The laws of the Medes and Persians could not be changed even by the king himself.

We also have to learn how to "draw near" to our King. We so easily disrespect our kind and loving king who has made a way open for us to come into His very throne room. We have a continual scepter extended to us. We have an open invitation. Let us draw near... and hear... and learn to obey. Let us learn the ways of the "Palace" and know how to approach our dear, loving and HOLY God. He shares his secrets with those who have a heart to receive, a heart to believe and a will to obey.

Those Nearest to Him

Jesus chose and discipled 12 men. He had the 70, the 120 and the crowds who followed him, but even of the 12 there were 3 or 4 who were "closest to him". These were the ones who saw him transfigured and who were invited to pray while with him in the garden in His most difficult hour. His closest disciples then, not surprisingly, became the pillars of the church. They knew his heart. They lay on his breast at dinner. They spoke with him on the way. They saw the miracles and he explained the parables to them alone.

The flow of authority in the Kingdom of God comes from the throne of God to those who are closest to Him. God chooses those closest to Him and He sends them. When we join ourselves to those whom He has sent and hear His heart in them, we can also enter into the flow of His Spirit with them. When we hear the words of truth they give and join our hands with theirs in doing THE WILL OF

GOD we will find ourselves in a river flowing out from the Throne of God.

In Ezekiel 47, the rivers flowing out into the desert became deeper as Ezekiel got closer to the desert and the seas of people who needed to be healed. "Rivers to swim in" flow through those closest to His throne, who have heard His heart and are moving out from there another thousand cubits and another thousand cubits; reaching out into the desert where the thirsty and the needy live. Many have missed this key and only want to stay near the throne. They can quickly become stale and ineffective because God's plan is to send us forth from the Throne Room.

Thy Will Be Done

Matt 21:28, Mark 11:21, Luke 20: 1 The chief priests, the scribes and the elders all came to Jesus with a question. These leaders represented the Sanhedrim's authority to question prophets and the 'judges in all matters legal' and they had come ask a question. "By what authority... and who gave you this authority to do these things?" Jesus asked them a question they did not want to answer and told them, "neither tell I you by what authority I do these things". Remember, Jesus had just cleansed the temple (who has the right to do that?) and cursed the fig tree (who has the power to do that?)

The question Jesus asked was about John, but it is also the answer to their question about authority, "The Baptism of John" Jesus asked, "did John and his parents make it up, or did God give it to him?" The baptism of John was a new thing; no one had ever practiced baptizing in a river out in public, this kind of repentance preaching had not been heard before either, where did it come from? John had never asked the "authorities" for permission to preach, so where did he get the right, ability and permission to do so? John grew up in the desert, not in seminary. Where did he learn these things from? **Luke 3:1-6** tells us **his word came from God** just as Isaiah had prophesied. So, his right, his ability, his power and his message all came from God; and so he had **the authority from God** to do it. God chose him, God separated him, God trained him, put His words in his mouth and then God released him to preach and baptize to prepare the way for Jesus coming.

Next, Jesus tells a parable of the two sons whom their father asked to work in the vineyard. One said he would and didn't (the priests) and one refused but did in the end (publicans and harlots). The question he asked points to the answer, "which one did the will of his father?" The obvious answer is, "the one who did the will of his father is the one who did the will of his father". But the point is; whatever resources the son needed to accomplish that task was at his disposal, up to all that the father had in his power. Whatever tools or manpower he needed were his. That son then also had the authority to direct the servants how the job must be done. He did not have to do it by himself or in his own strength alone. He had the authority to command all that was in his father's house to accomplish what his father wanted. This is a key to Kingdom authority. His Father asked him to do it.

Authority is found in obediently doing the will of the Father as a faithful steward of what He has given. Whatever He wants you to do; He will give you the ability, permission, and provision to do. He will open all of the doors of favor that are needed.

Understanding His Heart

We cannot do His will unless we understand His heart. When we obey in the little things, He gives us greater things to do. He reveals a little of the desires of His heart to us and we begin to move with "what we have in our hands" and then He shows us more of what is in His HEART.

Saul was used to giving orders and setting his own direction until he met Jesus on the road to Damascus. **Acts 9:6** "And he trembling and astonished said, **Lord, what wilt thou have me to do?** And the Lord said unto him, Arise, and go into the city, and **it shall be told thee what thou must do." He heard the heart of Jesus crying, "Why are you persecuting me?" Paul did not know God's heart, but when he discovered it he was a changed man.** The rest of Paul's life was spent in being told "what he must do". This is our life also if we ever want to be used by God in the way Paul was; hearing God's cry and doing His will.

God's heart is crying to have a people who will love Him, seek His face, know His heart and do His will. He desires to heal the nations and give rest to the weary. He longs to have men reconciled back to Himself. Will we get close enough to hear, and to feel HIS HEART?

Bringing His Kingdom to Earth Isaiah 58:12-14

Build the old waste places

The enemy comes to steal, kill and destroy but Jesus comes to give us life more abundantly. That abundant life in us begins to "make all things new". Places which have both spiritually and naturally been laid waste for generations will be built up through people filled with His Spirit and His Kingdom. He knows how to take waste places and make them a fruitful garden.

Isaiah 51:3 For the LORD shall comfort Zion: he will comfort all her waste places; and he will make her wilderness like Eden, and her desert like the garden of the LORD; joy and gladness shall be found therein, thanksgiving, and the voice of melody.

We have experience so many times when we went to an area in great need and cleaned and repaired in the natural that God brought freedom in the spiritual realms. In the Old Testament when God was honored and obeyed by His people Israel they were blessed and began to develop amazing cities, gardens, music and art.

Raise up the Foundations of Many Generations

People, families and communities are broken to their very foundations. Usually there is a long history of traumatic events that have rent the fabric of their society. They often carry an identity of victims and not victors. These foundations of lives and communities can be raised up again through the people of God. They can again have a firm foundation and a new identity on which to build which is based on forgiveness, reconciliation and restoration.

Repair the Breaches

Breaches are broken gaps in a stone wall which allows free access to predators and enemies. Sometimes we call them "open doors for the enemy". If people believe lies they will be easy targets. Psalms 91:4 Thy Truth is a shield and buckler (both used for protection from enemies). When people are missing principles of God's Kingdom they have spiritual gaps. Can we let Jesus in us fill in those gaps with Truth and anointing so people can stand in freedom?

Restore the Paths to Dwell In

A path is made from many feet going where they often go. It represents the habits of a people; everyday life. Where they live and how they live every day. For many people groups, there was once a path that their people dwelled in but they lost their way; like many of our dear Native Americans. For other people, it is hard to live without enough food, water, or resources. The 3 mile hike for water every morning to the muddy river in Nigeria made a path. The large commercial well which now serves over 10,000 people has shortened that path and the water does not make them sick. They now know there is a God in heaven that cares about them.

Restoring broken people, families, villages and communities is close to Father God's heart. Poor Health and nutrition shortens the path of a mother's life, her children will have to raise themselves. For people to live and thrive Jesus wants to bring them agriculture, sanitation, clean water, health and hygiene, small businesses, education and, community development.

Psalm 16:11 Thou wilt show me the path of life: in thy presence is fullness of joy; at thy right hand there are pleasures for evermore.

Psalm 23:3 He restores my soul: he leads me in the paths of righteousness for his name's sake.

God wants a people who can live in His presence and

walk in His paths of righteousness and bring His Kingdom to "all tribes and peoples and tongues".

Riding Upon the High Places of the Earth

Isaiah 58:14 Then shalt thou delight thyself in the LORD; and I will cause thee to ride upon the high places of the earth, and feed thee with the heritage of Jacob thy father: for the mouth of the LORD hath spoken it. (Deuteronomy 32:13)

This is a military term that refers to the honor given to a leader who has overcome and subdued even the strongholds of resistance in the high places. God said that He would, "cause us to ride" which implies that He will also cause us to win the victory, take the land, get the rule and live in safety. It is a place of honor and authority given to us by God Himself which comes after many battles are won. God is raising up "generals" in His army in the Earth; people, whom he has processed, tempered and who have been obedient, faithful, servant-leaders.

Habakkuk 3:19 The Lord God is my Strength, my personal bravery, and my invincible army; He makes my feet like hinds' feet and will make me to walk [not to stand still in terror, but to walk] and make [spiritual] progress upon my high places [of trouble, suffering, or responsibility]! (Amp) (2 Samuel 22:34, Psalm 18:33)

He is calling out people who have learned to walk in His ways and overcome the wicked one. Mature sons who have learned to work together with their Father and can carry responsibility. They are not afraid of trouble or suffering and are able to walk as sure footed as a deer upon high places. Their feet are guided by His voice; their hearts are fixed on Him.

The Lord Himself is their bravery. He Himself is their invincible army. They have overcome because of Him. They do not stand still in terror and do nothing, but they walk confidently led by Him. When the storm is all around they have learned to keep their eyes fixed on Jesus and they will not sink. They do not seek to do their own will or to be noticed by man. They live to please their Father and build His Kingdom. They ride upon the victories that have been won by the might and glory of their King.

Feeding on the Inheritance Promised to Jacob

God promised Jacob that **nations** would bow down to him.
Genesis 27:28-29, Genesis 28:14-15 Therefore God give you of the dew of heaven, and the fatness of the earth, and plenty of corn and wine: Let people serve you, **and nations bow down to you**: be lord over your brethren, and let your mother's sons bow down to you: cursed be every one that curses you, and blessed be he that blesses you. And your seed shall be as the dust of the earth, and you shall spread abroad to the west, and to the east, and to the north, and to the south: and in you **and in your seed (Jesus) shall all the families of the earth be blessed**. And, behold, I am with you, and will keep you in all places where ever you go, and will bring you again into this land; for I will not leave you, until I have done that which I have spoken to you of.

Many of the promises God gave to Jacob are fulfilled through Jesus, his "seed".

God promised His Son, Jesus, that He would be set up as a King among a holy people from every tribe, tongue and nation. They will be His possession, His bride and His inheritance. They will bring glory to His Father. Through them He will bring about the final victory over sin and Satan and death.

Psalm 2:6 Yet have I set my king upon my holy hill of Zion. 7 I will declare the decree: the LORD has said unto me, You are my Son; this day have I begotten you. **8** Ask of me, and I shall give you the heathen for your inheritance, and the uttermost parts of the earth for your possession.

God promises His Son that He would be set as King among His Holy people (Zion) and that He would be given people from every tribe, tongue and nation for His inheritance.(Rev 7:9) and that His enemies would become His footstool. (Psalm 110:1)

It is also His promise to those of us who are "with Him".

Revelation 17:14 These shall make war with the Lamb, and the Lamb shall overcome them: for he is Lord of lords, and King of kings: and they that are with him are the called, and chosen, and faithful.

It is also our right to ask for the spiritual keys that unlock nations of people who will be added to the inheritance of our King Jesus.

We are not collecting land, buildings, businesses and wealth. Lord forgive us for building our **own** international ministries. Lord change our motives and our understanding. We are gathering people from every tribe, tongue and people to be His inheritance. We are seeing strongholds broken over unreached souls so that they can come to know our precious Lord. We are demonstrating who **He** is and as we do, they will come to Him. They will be His bride, His inheritance, His body, His Kingdom. This is the fulfillment of His Father's promise; and we get to be "with Him" in the grand finale. **Lord we ask you for NATIONS!**

The Grand Finale

The curtains on the final act of all history cannot open until The Gospel of the Kingdom is preached in the entire world and the people witness something first hand. What do they see? They see the Love and the Provision and the Power of Almighty God through His people who are flowing together. God is going to have a body through which He is going to show this world Who He is. They are going to demonstrate to the world Who He truly is. Many will turn to Him when they see Him in Us.

Matthew 24:14 And this gospel of the kingdom shall be preached in all the world **for a witness** unto all nations; and then shall the end come.

What will the nations witness that will turn their hearts to Him? They will see Christ In Us. We, who are united, flowing together and demonstrating a Kingdom under the Most Excellent King. We who are lifting up the name of Jesus.

It will be demonstrated in the natural things as well as the spiritual.

In the natural realm, we believe God will give His people solutions to major world problems which no one else could solve; agriculture techniques for food shortages because of plagues and changes in the weather also medical breakthroughs in natural medicine. There will be many end time relief ministries raised up to respond to all of the earthquakes, wars, plagues and other disasters which are prophesied. Also there will be many ministries who are "building up the old waste places, repairing the breach and restoring paths to dwell in". His Provision will be amazing through His People for those in need. The Devil is busy setting up plans for death, devastation and destruction but God is working though us to make things glorious. He will bring Glory to Himself through US.

Spiritually, there will be gross darkness upon the people, but there will be many miracles and powerful demonstrations in the Earth through us. We will speak His words and He will bring the miraculous demonstrations. At His command we will prophesy and He will bring the signs following.

Acts 2:19-21 And I will perform wonders in the sky above and miraculous signs on the earth below, blood and fire and clouds of smoke. **20** The sun will be changed to darkness and the moon to blood before the great and glorious day of the Lord comes. **21** And then everyone who calls on the name of the Lord will be saved.

It may not be the large ministries who are most effective but rather many regular, unknown people who are sold out to Him will arise and begin to shine. In America, God will especially use the youth, the Native American and those who come from the "highways and the hedges" to bring in the harvest. Many who have been trained in the desert will bloom for all to see. He will be glorified.

The kings of the earth laugh at us now. They think we are weak and ineffective, and they may have good reason right now. But in that day, He will have the last laugh. (Ps 2:4-6) In the day that He sets His King upon His Holy hill of Zion (His People). Daniel saw a day in chapter 7 where the "separated ones" belonging to the Most High God would take and possess the Kingdom and all dominions and authorities will serve and obey Jesus.

Daniel 7:27 And the **kingdom** and the dominion and the greatness of the **kingdoms** under the whole heaven shall be given to the people of the saints of the Most High; his **kingdom** shall be an everlasting **kingdom,** and all dominions shall serve and obey him.' (ESV)

We can expect events in this world to become more and more turbulent, but we can be assured that **God has a plan** which **will cause Us** to "ride upon the high places of the Earth **with Him** and that **He will feed Us** with the heritage of Jacob our father:" (Isaiah 58:14)

Let us press in to these things. We say, "Yes, So be it Lord Jesus. Do it in our generation!"

FOR THE MOUTH OF THE LORD HATH SPOKEN IT

REVIEW: KINGDOM AUTHORITY

1. What best describes someone who is great in god's Kingdom?
a. They are leading many people
b. They are servant to all
c. They are the most excellent speakers'
d. All of the above

2. How many years did God train Moses?
a. 20
b. 40
c. 60
d. 80

3. God is the one who gives authority to whomever He wishes
a. True
b. False

4. God loves us to learn the ways of His "Palace" and know how to approach our dear, loving and HOLY God

a. True
b. False

5. The flow of authority in the Kingdom of God comes from the throne of God to those who are closest to Him
a. True
b. False

6. In Ezekiel 47, the river become more shallow once it flowed out into the desert
a. True
b. False

7. The greatest flow of Gods Spirit is found close to His throne
a. True
b. False

8. John the Baptists authority came from:
a. Being son of a temple priest
b. From the Sanhedrim
c. From Rabbinical training
d. From God's choosing and separating him

9. How can we get to be allowed to do greater things for God
a. By obediently doing the will of the Father
b. By faithfully doing what we know with what we have available
c. By knowing and moving with His heart
d. All of the above

10. . In the Old Testament when God was honored and obeyed by His people Israel they were blessed and began to develop amazing cities, gardens, music and art.
a. True
b. False

11. God's Kingdom includes agriculture, sanitation, clean water, health and hygiene, small businesses, education and, community development.
a. True
b. False

12. Riding upon the high places of the Earth is a military term which implies
a. God given victory by faithful obedient servant leaders
b. A place of honor given to those who have subdued even the strongholds
c. A place of authority that comes after many battles are won
d. All of the above

13. What best describes Mature Sons of the Father?
a. They have learned to work together with their Father and can carry responsibility
b. They are not afraid of trouble or suffering
c. Their feet are guided by His voice; their hearts are fixed on Him
d. All of the above

14. We have the right to ask for the spiritual keys that unlock nations of people who will be added to the inheritance of our King Jesus

a. True
b. False

15. In the Earth, there will be gross spiritual darkness upon the people, but there will be many miracles and powerful demonstrations through God's faithful ones.
a. True
b. False

REVIEW KEY: ISAIAH 58

Isaiah 58

1 b
2 b
3 c
4 a
5 b
6 b
7 c
8 a
9 d
10 b
11 b
12 b
13 c
14 a
15 c

Being Trained by The Spirit

1. c
2. a
3. a
4. d
5. b
6. d
7. c
8. b
9. b
10. b

Natural and Spiritual Flow Together

1. c
2. b
3. d
4. a
5. b
6. c
7. a
8. b
9. b
10. a
11. a
12. a
13. a
14. a
15. b

The Flow of God's Spirit

1. b
2. a
3. b
4. a
5. a
6. a
7. b
8. c
9. b
10. b
11. a
12. a
13. b
14. a
15. a

Ministering by the Spirit of the Lord

1. a
2. b
3. a
4. a
5. a
6. b
7. a
8. b
9. a
10. a

Christ in You, the Hope of Glory

1. b
2. a
3. d
4. b
5. b
6. b
7. c
8. c
9. b
10. b

God's Love Demonstrated

1. c
2. b
3. a
4. c
5. d
6. a
7. b
8. b
9. d
10. b
11. b
12. a
13. a
14. a
15. b

Dwelling Together in Unity

1. b
2. a
3. d
4. a
5. b
6. d
7. a
8. a
9. b
10. a
11. a
12. b
13. d
14. d
15. a
16. a

Kingdom Authority

1. b
2. d
3. a
4. a
5. a
6. b
7. b
8. d
9. d

10. a
11. a
12. d
13. d
14. a
15. a

Ezekiel's Wheel
The Making of a Man of God

Introduction

THE LATE FOUNDER of All Nations International, Rev. Agnes I. Numer, often taught on the vision of Ezekiel's Wheel. This vision is a beautiful description and revelation about **how to move with God.** It took many sessions before I finally understood and had a personal revelation of this incredible concept.

Thus began my study on the four gospels searching for all the attributes needed to function as a servant, an ox, as a son, an eagle, a brother, a man and as a person living with the revelation of our God given heritage as lion of the tribe of Judah.

The Vision of Ezekiel's Wheel exemplifies a call to move with the Spirit of the Lord to accomplish His plan and purpose on the earth.

In this study, we will compare each face of Ezekiel's Wheel - the Lion, the Ox, the Eagle and the Man - to the four Gospels. Although Jesus' character has many more than four facets, we will focus on the four found in Ezekiel Chapters 1, 2, 3.

What type of lives do we live? Do we live as Sons of God (the Eagle), as Servants of God (the Ox), or as Brothers of Jesus (the Man)? Do we even know who we are and that we can live by our God given heritage of the Lion of the tribe of Judah?

As you use this study may you feel propelled to allow God to remove those issues that prevent you from coming into His fullness and add to you what is lacking, that by His Spirit **you might be able to hear, see and respond to the**

moving of Ezekiel's wheel. And together you may flow with Him fully and see His Kingdom come.

Please enjoy the study and open your heart to experience the incredible journey of moving with God in Ezekiel's Wheel.

Ezekiel 1:12 "And they went every one straight forward: whither the spirit was to go, they went; and they turned not when they went."

Annella Whitehead

Chapter 25
REVELATION OF JESUS CHRIST

Prayer

FATHER, we thank You for the revelation of Jesus Christ. We thank You, Lord, that You're coming again very soon. Lord, You have so much to give us. You have so much to share with us. Drop by impartation into our hearts the vision that we may run by the Spirit of the living God. Thank You, Lord, for what You have for us by Your Spirit and in Your Name. Mighty God, we thank You and we ask You now Lord, to reveal Yourself to us that we may arise and go forth. Realizing the purpose that You've given us this revelation – that the Lord Jesus Christ shall arise in us, and You shall send us forth by the Spirit of God. Send us by the fullness of the Father in the fullness of time, to the ends of the earth, that we may see and behold the glory of the Lord. Thank You, Jesus. We praise You for this. In Your wonderful Name we ask this. Amen.

I. The Revelation of Jesus Christ In Us

The Lord's been speaking to me about Ezekiel. If you want a revelation of Jesus Christ open your hearts to receive it, as the Lord gives it to you through Ezekiel 1.

One time just before I moved to this house, the Lord gave me Ezekiel 1, 2, and 3. This was my training ground. Very mighty was the Word of the Lord and it changed my life. He changed it greatly through these chapters. Ezekiel 1 is the Revelation of Jesus Christ. It is Jesus Christ in us, in all His power and in all His glory. This chapter tells His whole story – when He went to heaven and when He was on earth. It's very wonderful. I'm going to share it with you through His Word.

Ezekiel 1 (KJV)

1 Now it came to pass in the thirtieth year, in the fourth month, in the fifth day of the month, as I was among the captives by the river of Chebar, that the heavens were opened, and I saw visions of God. 2 In the fifth day of the month, which was the fifth year of king Jehoiachin's captivity, 3 The word of the Lord came expressly unto Ezekiel the priest, the son of Buzi, in the land of the Chaldeans by the river Chebar; and the hand of the Lord was there upon him. 4 And I looked, and, behold, a whirlwind came out of the north, a great cloud, and a fire infolding itself, and a brightness was about it, and out of the midst thereof as the colour of amber, out of the midst of the fire.

5 Also out of the midst thereof came the likeness of four living creatures. And this was their appearance; they had the likeness of a man. 6 And every one had four faces, and every one had four wings. 7 And their feet were straight feet; and the sole of their feet was like the sole of a calf's foot: and

they sparkled like the colour of burnished brass. 8 And they had the hands of a man under their wings on their four sides; and they four had their faces and their wings. 9 Their wings were joined one to another; they turned not when they went; they went every one straight forward. 10 As for the likeness of their faces, they four had the face of a man, and the face of a lion, on the right side: and they four had the face of an ox on the left side; they four also had the face of an eagle. 11 Thus were their faces: and their wings were stretched upward; two wings of every one were joined one to another, and two covered their bodies.

12 And they went every one straight forward: whither the spirit was to go, they went; and they turned not when they went. 13 As for the likeness of the living creatures, their appearance was like burning coals of fire, and like the appearance of lamps: it went up and down among the living creatures; and the fire was bright, and out of the fire went forth lightning. 14 And the living creatures ran and returned as the appearance of a flash of lightning. 15 Now as I beheld the living creatures, behold one wheel upon the earth by the living creatures, with his four faces.

16 The appearance of the wheels and their work was like unto the colour of a beryl: and they four had one likeness: and their appearance and their work was as it were a wheel in the middle of a wheel. 17 When they went, they went upon their four sides: and they turned not when they went. 18 As for their rings, they were so high that they were dreadful; and their rings were full of eyes round about them four. 19 And when the living creatures went, the wheels went by them: and when the living creatures were lifted up from the earth, the wheels were lifted up.

20 Whithersoever the spirit was to go, they went, thither was their spirit to go; and the wheels were lifted up over

against them: for the spirit of the living creature was in the wheels. 21 When those went, these went; and when those stood, these stood; and when those were lifted up from the earth, the wheels were lifted up over against them: for the spirit of the living creature was in the wheels. 22 And the likeness of the firmament upon the heads of the living creature was as the colour of the terrible crystal, stretched forth over their heads above. 23 And under the firmament were their wings straight, the one toward the other: every one had two, which covered on this side, and every one had two, which covered on that side, their bodies. 24 And when they went, I heard the noise of their wings, like the noise of great waters, as the voice of the Almighty, the voice of speech, as the noise of an host: when they stood, they let down their wings.

25 And there was a voice from the firmament that was over their heads, when they stood, and had let down their wings. 26 And above the firmament that was over their heads was the likeness of a throne, as the appearance of a sapphire stone: and upon the likeness of the throne was the likeness as the appearance of a man above upon it. 27 And I saw as the colour of amber, as the appearance of fire round about within it, from the appearance of his loins even upward, and from the appearance of his loins even downward, I saw as it were the appearance of fire, and it had brightness round about. 28 As the appearance of the bow that is in the cloud in the day of rain, so was the appearance of the brightness round about. This was the appearance of the likeness of the glory of the Lord. And when I saw it, I fell upon my face, and I heard a voice of one that spake.

Ezekiel 2:1-5 (KJV)

1 And he said unto me, Son of man, stand upon thy feet,

and I will speak unto thee. 2 And the spirit entered into me when he spake unto me, and set me upon my feet, that I heard him that spake unto me. 3 And he said unto me, Son of man, I send thee to the children of Israel, to a rebellious nation that hath rebelled against me: they and their fathers have transgressed against me, even unto this very day.

4 For they are impudent children and stiffhearted. I do send thee unto them; and thou shalt say unto them, Thus saith the Lord God. 5 And they, whether they will hear, or whether they will forbear, (for they are a rebellious house,) yet shall know that there hath been a prophet among them.

II. King, Servant, Son of Man, Son of God

Jesus revealed Himself to Ezekiel who was one of God's major prophets in the land during the time of captivity. Even though Ezekiel was a prophet, it didn't mean he was going to escape captivity. **He sat among Israel as a captive.**

Ezekiel could not minister properly; He could not go to the Jewish people until he personally had the revelation of Jesus Christ. I'm sure he felt like he needed to do something, but it was hopeless without the Spirit of the Lord. **We must first have the revelation of Jesus Christ.** So here is this great prophet of God, sitting by the river Chebar in captivity, with a stubborn and rebellious people who did not want to hear from God and did not want to do what God wanted them to do. He's telling about a whirlwind that came out of the north and a great cloud and fire enfolding itself with a brightness that was around about it, out of the midst thereof as the colour of amber.

Then came the "likeness of four living creatures."

Now, remember, this was written in Ezekiel's day. This was not written after Jesus came - it was written before

Jesus came. This was when He wasn't yet a man, but He was the Son of God.

Let's look at Ezekiel 1:5-7:

5 Also out of the midst thereof came the likeness of four living creatures. And this was their appearance; they had the likeness of a man. 6 And every one had four faces, and every one had four wings. 7 And their feet were straight feet; and the sole of their feet was like the sole of a calf's foot: and they sparkled like the colour of burnished brass.

When you looked at the four living creatures, they had an appearance of a man. The four faces of the four creatures are Christ – Christ Jesus, the servant; Christ Jesus, the Son of Man; Christ Jesus, the Son of God; Christ Jesus, the King. Christ Jesus, bringing forth His body today in the revelation of Himself – Jesus, the Lion of the tribe of Judah; Jesus, the servant; Jesus, the Son of Man; Jesus, the Son of God.

The gospel of Matthew portrays Jesus as the Lion of the tribe of Judah for the Jews. The gospel of Mark portrays Jesus as a Servant, an ox. The gospel of Luke portrays Him as a man, the Son of Man. The gospel of John portrays Him as an eagle, the Son of God. Here is the completeness of Christ, on the earth, with the Word of God and with the purpose of God. The Lord brings them together and these creatures represent Jesus in full authority – King, Servant, Son of Man, Son of God – all things complete.

Jesus showed through these scriptures the five fold ministry that He had given to man. Ezekiel saw the hands of a man, these hands represent the hands of man. This was the work, the gifts, and the ministry of the Holy Spirit among the people. The gifts are given to bring the body of Christ into perfection. After the perfect one comes forth, then, the seven-fold spirit of God is going to take the place of the gifts.

The revelation was of Jesus. This is the ministry of Jesus Christ. They had straight feet, they had a purpose - they had a plan. Jesus has a purpose and a plan here in the revelation of Himself. The work that Jesus did when He walked the earth was done by the Son of Man... it was not done by the Son of God.

Remember what happened to Him when He was baptized in water? The Spirit of the Lord came upon Jesus. The Father acknowledged and the people recognized that Jesus was God's Son. He's shown here with a purpose, with a plan.

He was also known as Jesus, the Son of Man. The Father is the big wheel, Jesus is the little wheel, and **we are in Jesus**. Christ in man, man in Christ – the Father, the Son and us.

The eyes in the rim round about it are the seven spirits of God. We're in the middle of it with Jesus, with the gifts, with the ministry and the fullness of Jesus Christ. Something was happening to Ezekiel; he was receiving the revelation of Jesus Christ. The Spirit lifted Ezekiel and something began to happen. Out of this great wheel, the rings around it were full of eyes. The Spirit of the Lord, the Spirit of wisdom, the Spirit of knowledge, the Spirit of understanding, the Spirit of counsel, the Spirit of might and the Spirit of the fear of the Lord. **All at once this wheel began to move,** and it had the appearance of a wheel within a wheel. **As the Spirit began to move, it came to the throne of God and it came back to earth again.**

They had two wings that covered their body. Remember those four faces? They are the character, the nature, of Jesus Christ. He clothed them with true humility. The wings covered them, and they were not visible except for their faces. They were not exalted, but the appearance was the appearance of a man – that man is Jesus Christ, the Son of God, the Son of Man, the Servant, the King of kings and the Lord of lords.

As He brings us into this relationship with Him, there is **not going to be anything in you and I except Jesus.** We'll be clothed in Him, filled with Him, filled with His kingdom and filled with His glory.

As we allow Him to change our life, **we're going to ride on the high places of the earth.** I don't think we ought to waste any time, do you? Jesus wants everyone of us to be like He is. He paid the full price for us, and we need to enter in, and stop being stubborn, stop being rebellious. He wants to use us with the Spirit of the Lord in us, so that we can proclaim this Gospel of the Kingdom to the ends of the earth. It's not a dream, it's a reality. **No one is eligible to ride on this wheel unless they have permitted God to totally train them by the Spirit of the Lord.** There is no one sneaking in – no free rides. We all have to ride by the Spirit of the Lord. There is no halfway. There is no, "I'll do it my way," if you want to ride by the Spirit of the Lord and in His Wheel - you'll do it God's way.

He's giving us a mighty revelation of Jesus Christ and His work as He walked the earth. They rejected Him, but nevertheless He's the King of kings and the Lord of lords. They rejected Him because He was a servant, but, nevertheless, He is still servant to man. "He sits at the right hand of the Father ever making intercession for us." **We have to become a servant to Him.** We have to allow Him to take our life and move through us in the manner He chooses. **If we do not become a servant, we won't have a place with him.** If we don't allow His Spirit to move in us, we miss what He has for us. I'm not saying He doesn't want us to be intelligent. He is the greatest intelligence of all. I prefer personally to let Him be my intelligence. I prefer personally to let His wisdom be my wisdom. I prefer that His understanding and His knowledge be my understanding and knowledge, and His Spirit to have charge of me.

This is what He was doing for Ezekiel: He was preparing him for a special revelation of Jesus Christ. Not only to use him in that day, but for this day – for the revelation of Jesus Christ. The gifts are given here. The ministries are given here. The hands, the ministries, they call them the five-fold ministries. They're all represented here in Ezekiel 1. Everything about Jesus Christ as the man was given here to Ezekiel so that He could prepare us to go and do by the Spirit of the Lord.

What God had for us to do is very simple, it's not complicated. The complication is what we do with it. If we yield to Him, we too, will receive the revelation of Jesus Christ. You see, it's not just receiving it, it's the Lord preparing us that He is going to do something through us out there.

III. We're Living In The Day of the Fullness of Christ

My heart was being stirred by the Word of God. I believe **God wants to give us everything** and I don't believe He wants to hold back anything. What I see in the Word, many people don't see, and maybe they see a lot of things I don't see.

One thing I see is the revelation of Jesus Christ, when he said to His disciples, "Tarry ye until you be endowed with power from on high". It was then that he gave us the Holy Ghost and fire. He also gave us the gifts and the ministry of the Holy Spirit. But the Word says that the gifts were by measure. There's also another part where He said, "The Spirit of the Lord is upon me and the Spirit of wisdom..." (Isaiah 11:2) What He is saying is that He wants us to have **Jesus in us so He can fulfill everything through us that the father sent Him to do – with no limitations.** We can have His Spirit without measure. We're living in that day of the fullness of time, in the fullness of the father, and that's what Ezekiel 1 is talking about.

The full revelation of Jesus is when we lay aside our brightness, our intelligence, our everything. Those things don't matter. What really matters is that Jesus lives in us and that we receive from Him the full revelation of Jesus Christ.

The Lord told me when He brought me to the desert, "I'm going to take out of you the traditions and bondages of man. I'm going to teach you My ways." and then this is what He gave me. Ezekiel 1, 2 and 3.

We're living in the day of the fullness of Christ, the fullness of the father, in the fullness of time. We're going to allow Him to reveal Himself as he revealed Himself to Ezekiel – in the glory of the Lord, the awesomeness of His presence, and in the fullness of God. So we can go to heaven? No. There is a purpose, but God didn't give it to them. He gave it to us. Why? Because He has a plan for us. This plan is to take this gospel of the revelation of Jesus Christ in the fullness of time, in the fullness of the Father, in the full plan of God in the last days. We have to allow the Lord to give us the revelation of the great and mighty Christ. We have to be first a servant. We have to get rid of our pride. We have to permit Him to clean us out so there's nothing there. Then the brightness of the glory of His presence will then fill our temples, and we'll be ready to go with Him.

There must be a reason why there is a wheel within a

wheel. In John 17, Jesus prayed a prayer for us. It was a mighty prayer, that we might be in Him and He in us and He in the father and the Father in us. Ezekiel 1 is preparing us to fit in that place in the Lord. Jesus gave us His kingdom. What does His kingdom consist of? Love, peace, joy, righteousness, holiness. There is no law against it. Jesus said, "I give you this that you might take my love to the heathen." Sometimes you think, "Well, the heathen are going to go without God", but remember, that was not God's plan. He sent His Son into the world to redeem the whole world. The kings and the rulers of the earth decided they were not going to allow the people to know Him. I tell you, **God has a secret, and it's mighty** because it's the full revelation of Jesus Christ. When He's finished with us, if we will permit Him to do it, we're going to find something that we didn't know. He has made us as He is in this world. Then we can stand in the day of judgment, and we can boldly stand there because we're like Jesus.

He's giving us the privilege of that revelation in us so that we can ride upon the high places of the earth with him. If we obey Him, we will have it, and we will be riding in the glory of the Lord.

IV. A Vision – The Realm of Eternity

God gave me a vision. He lifted me in the Spirit and took me into the realm of eternity before time was. I was sitting in a home in India at a dinner table talking to a young man. The man parents were sitting with us and they were Catholics. I was sitting there and all at once, this young man asked me a question. He said, "Any religion all right, if you believe in it, isn't it?" And all at once, I don't know what happened to me. I was still talking to them at the table but I do not know what I said to them, because all at once, I was experiencing something in the Heavens.

I was taken by the Lord into the realm of eternity, before the creation of man. I heard the Son discussing with the Father that He would be willing to become the Lamb that was slain before the foundation of the world. They discussed the creation of the world, the creation of man and then Jesus decided that He would go and become a little baby and become the Son of Man.

There was one thing that down through the years, I said to the Father. "Father, why do You permit the people to treat You the way they treat you?" He gave me the Word in Psalms and He said, "the children of Israel provoked Him to anger and He took away His Shekinah presence from them." He has caused His strength to go into captivity and His glory into the enemy's hands. He said, "**The time will come when I'm going to take My strength out of captivity and My glory out of the enemy's hands, and I'm going to show the world who I am.**"

As I was witnessing these things in the heavens, I saw the **heart of God, the Father,** and I saw the price that He paid to let His beloved Son come to be cursed, blasphemed and die for a people who didn't want Him. I felt the heartbreak of the Father. I felt the heaviness, and I felt the great love of God that He had for His Son. How difficult it must have been. I think that's why it says in John, "For God so loved the world, that He gave His only begotten Son that whosoever believeth in Him should not perish but have everlasting life." John 3:16

After the Lord had shown me this, He said, "I will not hold anybody guiltless who refuses my Son." I don't know what I said to this young man, but I'm sure I told him what the Lord said. I didn't know what had gone on at the table so I turned to my friend and I asked, "Tell me, what did I say?" She said, "I don't know, but it was wonderful."

To this day, I don't know what I said at that table that day, but the glory of the Lord was over me. It was a little difficult coming down to that table and among the people because my heart cried out, "Father, You know how much You love Your Son." We talk about how much Jesus loves us but the Father also went through a lot of things for us to have His Son. Now we're receiving the revelation of His Son.

This same Jesus became the Son of Man that He might draw us unto Himself, that we might have Him revealed to us, so that He can use us. He said, "Greater things than these shall you do because I go to My Father." You see, we're living in the end of time. We're living in the fullness of time, in the fullness of the Father. Jesus is getting us ready for the mighty flowing forth of His glory, the glory of the Lord, Jesus the Son of Man.

V. God Is Transforming Our Lives

When Ezekiel received the revelation of Jesus Christ, from that moment forward He went in the power of the Spirit. He never went in His own power. He never went thinking He was doing something. He went knowing that God was moving and speaking through him. He went knowing that it was Jesus moving and speaking through him. It is not who we are, it is the revelation of Jesus.

Remember, we're living in a day others have longed to live in, but consider who we are. We're not anybody, and yet He's going into the prisons, He's going into the streets, He's going among the gangs, He's going to transform our lives by the revelation of Himself, by the Spirit of the Lord.

Then He's going to make us mighty men and women of God because we're going to arise in the fullness of the Spirit. After he received the revelation of Jesus Christ, Ezekiel never did anything **except that he moved by the Spirit of the Lord.**

It's very important for us to allow God to change us so that we can be filled with His Spirit - the way He wants us to be. We are no match for these things. In 2 Peter, Chapter 1, we see how God is processing our life to make us as He is, filling us with His love, so that His love through us reaches out to a dying world. Read it in the King James Version as other versions leave this revelation out.

2 Peter 1 is the changing of our life into His likeness and into His nature. I believe when we get into the realm of completeness in Him, the wisdom of God is just going to flow through us, the knowledge of God is just going to flow through us and the understanding of God is just going to flow through us. How can we be in God and in Christ, and Christ in us, and not know anything about God? He is going to have charge over us so we can move by His Spirit.

He told me when He gave me the revelation of Isaiah 58 that He allowed men to acquire riches, and when He told them where to put it, they would put it there. He's given people hidden riches in the secret places. He's given them inventions. He's given them all kinds of things for this hour by the hand of God. He kept it from the world, and He's given it to those that move by His Spirit in Ezekiel 1.

Jesus said, "Come unto me, all ye that labor and are heavy laden and I will give you rest. Take my yoke upon you and learn of Me, for My yoke is easy and My burden is light." Matthew 11:28

We can fly away, but we're flying in the hour of Ezekiel's wheel by the Spirit of the Lord. I trust this has dropped in your hearts. We don't have much time, but Jesus has a plan. He'll clean us up quickly, and He'll reveal Himself quickly. He'll change our lives.

Now, Jesus says, you're ready to run. You'll move when I move, and when I don't move, you don't move – you let your wings down and you rest. When He's ready to move, get ready to move. We move with Him. We don't get anxious because we've been trained by Him through the gifts, through the ministry; and, more importantly we've been trained by the Spirit of the Living God. **It was the Spirit of the Living God that was upon Ezekiel and He, today, has called us to have the Spirit of the Lord upon us.**

I feel the awesomeness of what God has planned for us if we will permit Him to change our life. We will see Him as Ezekiel saw Him, then we will know that wherever the Spirit goes, that we're going to go; and when the Spirit doesn't go, we're not going to go. We're going to rest in Him. The work is mighty. Jesus in us, us in Jesus, in the middle of the wheel. We're living in the hour that God wants to use every one of us by the full revelation of Jesus Christ – **that we might ride in Ezekiel's wheel with Him.**

VI. We Have the Privilege to Walk

Then shalt thou delight thyself in the Lord; and I will cause thee to ride upon the high places of the earth, and feed thee with the heritage of Jacob thy father: for the mouth of the Lord hath spoken it. Isaiah 58:14

We don't need anything else... He spoke to Ezekiel, "Son of Man, go and give them the revelation of Jesus Christ." Give it to them that they may take it to the ends of the earth.

Everything looks to the contrary, but it's not. If we

will permit Him to remove from our life everything that is not of God, then His Spirit shall have the rule and reign in our life. Just as surely as this is written, it will come to pass for you.

I believe that when we come into what God has for us through the revelation of Jesus Christ that God the Father is in us and Jesus is in us and we're in them. Then we can draw our resources from heaven. We can draw our knowledge from Him. It's not our knowledge. I don't want any knowledge – all I want is God's knowledge; and when He wants me to know something; and when He wants me to have His wisdom, I want it. When He wants me to have His understanding, I want it. When He wants me to have His direction or His counsel, I want it. **This is exactly what Ezekiel's wheel is - God moving in us and us moving in Him.**

We have Jesus in the revelation of His Spirit, in the fullness of time, in the fullness of the father and in the fullness of His kingdom. How can we turn that aside? How can we choose our own greatness and try to figure everything out with our wisdom? He has it all for us, when He's ready to give it to us. Not when we're ready to take it, because we probably wouldn't have the wisdom to handle it right.

Isaiah 11:1-6

And there shall come forth a rod out of the stem of Jesse, and a Branch shall grow out of his roots: 2 And the spirit of the Lord shall rest upon him, the spirit of wisdom and understanding, the spirit of counsel and might, the spirit of knowledge and of the fear of the Lord; 3 And shall make him of quick understanding in the fear of the Lord: and he shall not judge after the sight of his eyes, neither reprove after the hearing of his ears:

4 But with righteousness shall he judge the poor, and reprove with equity for the meek of the earth: and he shall smite the earth: with the rod of his mouth, and with the breath of his lips shall he slay the wicked. 5 And righteousness shall be the girdle of his loins, and faithfulness the girdle of his reins.

6 The wolf also shall dwell with the lamb, and the leopard shall lie down with the kid; and the calf and the young lion and the fatling together; and a little child shall lead them.

Isaiah 11:10-11

10 And in that day there shall be a root of Jesse, which shall stand for an ensign of the people; to it shall the Gentiles seek: and His rest shall be glorious. 11 And it shall come to pass in that day, that the Lord shall set His hand again the second time to recover the remnant of His people, which shall be left, from Assyria, and from Egypt, and from Pathros, and from Cush, and from Elam and from Shinar, and from Hamath, and from the islands of the sea.

That's what God is doing today, isn't it? **He has a work to be done by us,** by the full revelation of Jesus Christ. I'm glad for the Spirit of the Lord. It is by His Spirit that He wants us to receive His Word as it is written. Today, we have the privilege to have everything that the Father gave to Jesus - and to walk in it. **Jesus came as the Son of Man, but He left us as the King of Glory.** He fulfilled everything that the Father gave Him to do that we might be filled with the fullness of the Father.

He said, "I set before you a door that no man can close". We're living in that hour – but it has to be God's way. We have to allow Him to do everything quickly so he can send us to do this work which He's called us to do.

I firmly believe the Lord wants to use the nationals in

their own countries, quickly, mightily, to minister to the people by the Spirit of the Lord. **Let's remember Ezekiel could do nothing until he received the revelation of Jesus Christ.** Everywhere he went, everything he did, was by the Spirit of the Lord.

We're believing God. He's greater than all the powers of Satan. He's a mighty God, and we need to let Jesus have His way, by His Spirit, and **not to try to do it our way.** God is preparing us for a mighty work in Him. Now it has begun. It's already started. We need to prepare ourselves to move in the fullness of His Spirit to obey Him, that we might enjoy the fullness of the Father in our life – so that He can do the mighty works. We can't say what those works are because they're past our understanding. We're going to marvel as it comes, knowing that it is God. Amen.

The Revelation of Jesus Christ – Message by Rev. Agnes I. Numer

REVIEW: REVELATION OF JESUS CHRIST

1. The four faces of the creatures are Christ Jesus the: __ angel __servant __Son of God __Son of Man __Son of Mary __King __Human __Son of God __Savior

2. In Ezekiel Chapter 1, what is the Revelation of Jesus Christ? It is Jesus Christ ____ ____, in all His ____ and in all His ____.

3. "and they went every one straight ____ : whither the spirit was to go, they ____ ; and they ____ ____ when they went."

4. "As He brings us into into relationship with Him, there is not going to be anything in you and I, except Jesus."
5. What makes us eligible to ride in the wheel? __ asking God to ride in the wheel, __ getting trained to ride the wheel by reading the Bible, __ permitting God to totally train them by the Spirit of the Lord, __ jumping inside the wheel

6. "Tarry on until you be endowed with power from on high." What is the power that comes from "on high"? __ Spirit of Discernment __ Spirit of Wisdom __ Holy Spirit __ Spirit of the age

7. We hate to be first a ____ . We have to get rid of our ____.

8. What does the kingdom of God consist of? (Check all that apply) __ Joy __Righteousness __Love __Pride __Peace __Arrogance __Holiness __Education

9. "When He's finished with us, if we will permit Him to do it, we are going to find that He has made us comfortable as He is in this world."
a. True
b. False

10. "Jesus is getting us ready for the mighty flowing forth of His glory, the glory of the Lord, Jesus the Son of Man."
a. True
b. False

11. When Ezekiel ____ the ____ of Jesus Christ, from that moment forward He went in the ____ ____ ____ ____. He went knowing that it was ____ moving and ____ through him. He went knowing that it was ____ moving and ____ through him.

12. "It is very important for us to allow God to change us so that we can be filled with His Spirit."
a. True

b. False

13. Then shalt thou _____ _____ in the Lord; and I will _____ thee with the _____ of Jacob thy father: for the _____ of the Lord hath spoken it.

14. "If we don't permit Him to remove from our life everything that is not of God, then His spirit shall have rule and reign in our life."
a. True
b. False

15. God is _____ us for a _____ work in Him. We _____ ourselves to move in the _____ of his spirit to _____ Him, that He might enjoy the _____ of the _____ in our life.

16. To be His servant, what do we need to get rid of? __ hate, __ anger, __ pride, __joy

Chapter 26

MARK - FACE OF THE OX

Mark - Face of the Ox

WE LOOK through Mark's Gospel at what Jesus did as a servant. Servants perform duties for others, making sure that other's needs are taken care of before their own.

The ox was considered a beast of burden. Often a yoke was put on the ox so that large loads could be carried or pulled by them.

In this study we are preparing ourselves with the attributes of a servant so that we can move with the Spirit in the Wheel.

Preparation

Mark 1: 35 "And in the morning, rising up a great while before day, he went out, and departed into a solitary place, and there prayed."

Servants prepare ahead of time often a 'great while' before others. This preparation of serving with God requires the attribute of prayer so that we can know the direction of the Master (God) to move with Him in the wheel.

Discernment

Mark 2: 5-11.Jesus heard from the master that the paralyzed man needed to know first of all that his sins were forgiven. This is what was preventing him from walking. In V8 Jesus also discerns (perceived) in his spirit that there were questions in the hearts of the scribes. Because of the discernment he was able to bring healing to the paralyzed man causing him to fully recover and also correctly answer the scribes.

Obedience

Mark 2: 14-17 Jesus calls Levi (a tax collector) to be a disciple and then has a meal at his home with other publicans and sinners. The Scribes and the Pharisees question why he eats with them. The wheel was moving to show a Pharisee the truth about God. Jesus obeyed the moving of the wheel despite the religious separation. Jesus answers their question V17 "The sick needed a physician and sinners to be called to repentance".

Do not become religious

Mark 2:19 And Jesus said unto them, Can the children of the bridechamber fast, while the bridegroom is with them? as long as they have the bridegroom with them, they cannot fast.

Servants cannot become ridged in how they do things (become religious). Servants (disciples) obey the direction of the Master (Father) for each situation. Jesus obeyed His Father's heart, He moved by the Spirit in the Wheel.

Mark 2: 27 And he said unto them, The sabbath was made for man, and not man for the sabbath: 28 Therefore the Son of man is Lord also of the sabbath.

Who is the family?

Mark 3:31-34 31 There came then his brethren and his mother, and, standing without, sent unto him, calling him. 32 And the multitude sat about him, and they said unto him, Behold, thy mother and thy brethren without seek for thee. 33 And he answered them, saying, Who is my mother, or my brethren? 34 And he looked round about on them which sat about him, and said, Behold my mother and my brethren!

In this passage Jesus is expanding our thoughts and actions as a servant. Jesus did not reject his mother and brethren, but uses the opportunity to illustrate who is family. V35 "For whosoever shall do the will of God, the same is my brother, and my sister, and mother". A servant does not get to choose his family, as servants we serve those who our Father has put before us to minister to.

Hearing

Mark 4:24 "And he said unto them, Take heed what ye hear: with what measure ye mete, it shall be measured to you: and unto you that hear shall more be given". Is your heart receptive to hearing? The parable of sower is looking at the receptiveness to the word of God.

Trusting

Mark 4: 26-29 Sow and wait for the harvest then harvest immediately ... This is the kingdom. Trust in the sower that the fruit will come forth at the right time. We only need to wait for the maturity, then immediately harvest the completed fruit.

Have Faith

Mark 4: 40 "And he said unto them, "Why are ye so fearful? How is it that ye have no faith?" The storm was not concerning Jesus, but the disciples were terrified. As servants we need to have faith in where the spirit leads us in the wheel. Jesus said to go over to the other side. If he is in the boat, they should surely get there despite the very strong storm.

So often we get moving in the direction we are to go, knowing and believing it is the direction to move in with the Lord in the boat (Wheel). On the way there is a storm, or a problem that terrifies us. Are we going to give up or go back or are we going to go to the other side? Do we trust that we have heard, and have faith that we will get through the storm?

Rest

Mark 6:31 "And he said unto them, 'Come ye yourselves apart into a desert place, and rest a while: for there were many coming and going; and they had no leisure so much as to eat'"

In chapter 6 Jesus sent His disciples out with instructions to do what He had taught them. Mark 6:12 And they went out, and preached that men should repent. 13 And they cast out many devils, and anointed with oil many that were sick, and healed them. They also had to bury John the Baptist. Jesus himself tells them 'to come apart and rest.'

Ezekiel 1:21 'when the spirit moved they moved, when those stood they stood.'

Rest is important, we must rest when the Spirit rests.

Let's Review:

Take some time to look at the Attributes of a servant that you have already studied. Preparation - have you purposed to pray, so that your Discernment will be true? Are you Obeying the leading of the Spirit of the Lord? Are you moving in the wheel with Grace and Truth (righteousness), not just following the law? Your Family-does it encompass those that God has sent you to serve? Are you Hearing so that God can Trust you with His Harvest? Are you increasing in Faith that the Spirit is leading you in the right direction? Are you learning to rest when the 'wheel' stands still?

Allow the Lord to develop these servant attributes in your life so that you can move by the Spirit in the wheel.

Don't just check [ ] each one off like a list. Don't file them away and think that you have passed a test. These servant attributes are what we need to be able to move in the Spirit in the wheel. It is a continuing work in our lives.

Ezekiel 1:20-21 "Whithersoever the spirit was to go, they went, thither was their spirit to go; and the wheels were lifted up against them: for the spirit of the living creature was in the wheel. When those went, these went; and when those stood, these stood; and when those were lifted up from the earth, the wheels were lifted up against them, for the spirit of the living creature was in the wheels."

The late Rev. Agnes Numer would say when teaching on Ezekiel's Wheel "Get ready for the ride of your life."

Read: Ezekiel Chapters 2 & 3

Compassion

We have learned about REST. Servants need to rest when the Spirit rest (in the wheel). Jesus and his disciples got in a boat to get away from the people to rest, then…. Mark 6:34 "And Jesus, when he came out, saw much people, and was moved with compassion toward them, because they were as sheep not having a shepherd: and he began to teach them many things." This is the nitty gritty of 'wheel' life. God's timing is not our timing. His main interest is to attend to the wellbeing of His children.

At times compassion will move, and rest needs to wait, because the circumstances cannot wait. V35-44 you will see that Jesus not only taught them spiritually, but provided food for them also.

Notice that Jesus taught the whole day, this was not just a short time of 'extra' serving. Remember 'Ezekiel 1:20, 21 'When those went, these went; and when those stood, these stood..."

Note: This attribute of compassion is perhaps the turning point from just being a servant to being a 'servant son'. Denying ones' self and obedience can be self-sacrificial - we can accomplish them by ourselves perhaps - but, when we have the attribute of compassion and move on it, this is when we choose the Father's heart and we become Sons.

Servant Heart

Mark 8:31-38. A servant has to be obedient to his purpose in life. An ox carries burdens for others without question and the ox does not get to consider its own needs.

Jesus explains to the people His purpose on earth. V31b "...the Son of man must suffer many things, and be rejected of the elders, and of the chief priests, and scribes, and be killed, and after three days rise again." When Peter's rebukes him, Jesus's response is V33b "For thou savourest not the things of God, but the things that are of men."

Mark 9:33, 34, 35 and 10:42-45. The dispute on who will be first and then Jesus response. 9:35 "And he sat down and called the twelve, and saith unto them, If any man desire to be first, the same shall be last of all, and servant of all." 10:45 "For even the Son of man came not to be ministered unto, but to minister, and to give his life a ransom for many."

Forgive

Mark 11:25, 26. As a burden bearer (the ox), the servant can be subject to overuse. This happens when we serve in our own strength and we do not move when the spirit moves. This can cause us to be angry and bitter which can lead to unforgiveness. Mark 11:25-26 "And when ye stand praying, forgive if ye have ought against any: that your Father also which is in heaven may forgive you your trespasses. But if you do not forgive, neither will your Father which is in heaven forgive your trespasses." We need to forgive so we can be free to move in the majestic wheel.

Love

Mark 12:28-31. A scribe asks Jesus this question - what is the first commandment of all? Jesus's reply is "Hear, O Israel; The Lord our God is one Lord: And thou shalt love the Lord thy God with all thy heart, and with all thy soul, and with all thy mind; and with all thy strength; this is the first commandment. And the second is like, namely this, Thou shalt love thy neighbour as thyself. There is none other commandment greater than these."

The scribe responds with this statement. 12:32, 33 "And to love him with all the heart and with all the understanding, and with all the soul, and with all the strength, and to love his neighbor as himself, is more than all whole burnt offerings and sacrifices"

Burnt offerings and sacrifices were made for sin atonement and also love offerings to God. God talks about sweet smelling sacrifices, acceptable to Him.

To love the Lord our God with ALL our soul, and our neighbour with ALL/AS ourselves, would make the

WHOLE burnt offering. This would be acceptable to the Lord, a 'sweet smell'.

The whole is: All of the heart, All of the soul, All of the mind, and All of the strength. This is the Love of a servant to the Master.

Giving

Read Mark 12: 43-44 "And he called unto him his disciples, and saith unto them, Verily I say unto you, That this poor widow hath cast more in, than all they which have cast into the treasury: For all they did cast in of their abundance; but she of her want did cast in all that she had, even all her living." The widow gave all that she could.

A servant's giving is sacrificial. Are you giving out of your abundance or out of your need?

Watch and Pray

Read Mark 13: 34- 37 The Master goes on a journey and gives Authority to his servants, and to every man a job or work to do and commanded the porter to watch.
V35"Watch ye therefore: for ye know not when the master of the house cometh, at even or at midnight, or at the cock crowing, or in the morning."

Read Mark 14: 4-38 "Watch and pray lest you enter into temptation, the spirit truly is ready, but the flesh is weak."

Work keeps us busy and about our Master's business. Watching for the master's return keeps us alert to the future. Watching and Praying keeps us from entering into temptation.

These are attributes that transform us from servant to son.

Don't follow the crowd.

Mark 14:3-9 3 And being in Bethany in the house of Simon the leper, as he sat at meat, there came a woman having an alabaster box of ointment of spikenard very precious; and she break the box, and poured it on his head. 4 And there were some that had indignation within themselves, and said, Why was this waste of the ointment made? 5 For it might have been sold for more than three hundred pence, and have been given to the poor. And they murmured against her. 6 And Jesus said, Let her alone; why trouble ye her? She hath wrought a good work on me. 7 For ye have the poor with you always, and whensoever ye will ye may do them good: but me ye have not always. 8 She hath done what she could: she is come aforehand to anoint my body to the burying. 9 Verily I say unto you, Wheresoever this gospel shall be preached throughout the whole world, this also that she hath done shall be spoken of for a memorial of her.

Our focus is on the wellbeing of people. Jesus was visiting an outcast, Simon the leper, and a woman was anointing Him with expensive oil that others watching thought could have been used for a more noble purpose, like feeding the poor.

Helping people find salvation into God's kingdom is what is more important than what the crowd thinks or how people are showing their gratitude.

Be guided by the Spirit moving in the wheel rather than the traditions of man. Become more aware of where the Spirit is moving and go where He is going.

Moving with the Spirit, is not always with a crowd or majority.

Become as the Master

Mark 16:15-18 "And he said unto them, "Go ye into all the world, and preach the gospel to every creature. He that believeth and is baptized shall be saved; but he that believeth not shall be damned; And these signs shall follow them that believe; in my name shall they cast out devils; they shall speak with new tongues; They shall take up serpents; and if they drink any deadly thing, it shall not hurt them; they shall lay hands on the sick, and they shall recover."

As we take on the attributes of a servant, we learn the master's ways. We learn to see the needs of others and with willingness serve them.

We will then be Sons of God, able to move with the Spirit in the wheel as the Master (God).

We will move when the Spirit moves, and rest when He rests, and it will be the greatest ride of our lives!

Ezekiel 1:12 "And they went every one straight forward: whither the spirit was to go."

REVIEW: MARK - FACE OF THE OX

1. Servants prepare ahead of time, often a "_____ _____". This preparation of serving _____ God requires the attributes of _____ so that He can know the _____ of the _____ God to _____ with Him in the _____.
2. Servants (_____) obey the _____ of the Master (_____) for _____ situation.
3. A servant does not get to choose his family. As servants we _____ those who our Father has _____ _____ _____ to minister to.
4. "As servants, we need to have faith in where the Spirit leads us in the wheel." __True __False
5. "For even the son of man came _____ to be _____ unto, but minister, and to give His life a _____ for many."
6. "And when ye stand praying _____ if ye have _____ against any, that your Father which is in heaven may forgive you your trespasses."
7. Watching and praying keeps us from entering into temptation. __True __False

8. Moving with the _____ is not always with a _____ or _____.
9. As we take on the _____ of a servant we _____ the Master's way.
10. "We see the needs of others and with unwillingness serve them." __True __False

Chapter 27

JOHN - SON OF GOD

John's Gospel - the Face of the Eagle

THE PURPOSE of this study is to develop the attributes of a Son of God. To mature and acknowledge who we are in God, so that we can move in that authority in the 'wheel' with the Spirit of God.

We will look through John's gospel at what Jesus did as the Son of God. The Nature of the son, His mission and His understanding of who He was... the Son of the most High God.

Attributes of a Son of God

- Receive him
- Born Again
- Grace and truth
- Zeal for the home
- Obedience
- Believe
- Have righteous judgment
- Continue in the word
- Abide
- Work while it is Day
- Give your life
- Be humble
- Be Fruitful & love
- Ask
- Speak Openly
- Fulfill your purpose - Son of God

Receive Him

John 1:4 "In him was life and the life was the light of men." V.9 "That was the true light which lighteth every man that cometh into the world." V 12 "But as many as received him, to them gave he power to become the sons of God, even to them that believe on his name:"

Before we discover the attributes and functions of a son of God we must receive him as Lord and believe on His name. It is only then that we get the power and ability to take on the attributes and be sons.

Have your received Jesus Christ into your life as Lord

and Savior? Are you a son? You must receive Him as Lord of your life, to have power and ability to become complete sons.

Born Again

John 3:5-7 Jesus answered, "Truly, truly, I say to you, unless one is born of water and the Spirit he cannot enter into the kingdom of God. 6"That which is born of the flesh is flesh, and that which is born of the Spirit is spirit. 7"Do not be amazed that I said to you, 'You must be born again.'

John 3:16 "For God so loved the world that he gave his only begotten Son, that whosoever believeth in him should not perish, but have everlasting life." John 1:33, 34 ...Upon whom thou shalt see the Spirit descending, and remaining on him, the same is he which baptizeth with the Holy Ghost. 34And I saw, and bare record that this is the Son of God.

Our new birth gives us the capacity not to condemn, but through our lives bring people to salvation. Being a Son of God.

Grace and Truth

John 1:17 "For the law was given by Moses, but grace and truth came by Jesus Christ."

Grace means unmerited divine assistance. Truth means the real or true facts about something. Christ came to fulfill the Law of Moses by grace and truth.

Grace and Truth by Jesus Christ (direction from the Father) must become an integral attribute of our character. This is a principal foundation of being a son.

Our service to man must be by Grace and Truth, the fulfillment of the Law.

Zeal for the House

John 2:16, 17 "And he said unto them that sold doves, Take these things hence; make not my Father's house a house of merchandise." And his disciples remembered that it is written, "The zeal of thine house has eaten me up."

God's house should be kept sanctified? This house is not only the building of worship, but also our living temple that we have invited God to live in- ourselves.

If our house is not filled with the righteousness of the Father we will not be able to see clearly when the Spirit is moving in the wheel. We will be blinded because our house is not pure.

As sons we need to be jealous for the Holiness of God's house.

Obedience

John 4:32- 34 "My meat is to do the will of him that sent me, and to finish (complete) his work." Jesus obeyed his father's leading by speaking to this Samaritan woman and thereby bringing her whole village to God's saving grace. John 4:35-38

John 5:17 "My Father worketh hitherto, and I work." This statement comes after Jesus heals the lame man at the pool on the sabbath. The Jews want to kill him because it is not the law to work on the sabbath.

John 5:19, 20 "Verily, verily, I say unto you, The Son can do nothing of himself; but what he seeth the Father do: for what things so ever he doeth, these also doeth the Son likewise."

John 5:30 "I can of mine own self do nothing: as I hear, I judge: and my judgement is just; because I seek not mine own will, but the will of my Father which hath sent me."

Let's Review:

When moving in the wheel, obedience is a key. We are learning Kingdom ways that are not man ways. Imagine being led by the Spirit of the Lord, "wheel moving", in a similar circumstance like speaking to the Samaritan woman at the well?

Maturity is also necessary along with obedience, so we can be trusted with situations similar to this.

Develop the attribute of obedience, so that you can move in the wheel by God's Grace and Truth, to guide others to salvation.

Obedience is not bondage - it is the Son's good pleasure to obey the Father. Joy, comfort and satisfaction are the reward when we move with our Father in the 'wheel'.

Believe

John 6:22-28 Wuest Translation

V26-29 "Jesus answered them and said, "Most assuredly, I am sent to you, you are seeking me, not because you saw attesting miracles, but because you ate of the loaves and were satisfying filled. Stop working for the food which perishes, but work for the food which abides for life eternal which the Son of Man will give you, for this One the Father sealed, even God." Then they said to him, "what are we to do as a habit of life that we may continually be working the works of God?" Answered Jesus and said to them, "This is the work of God that you continually be believing on Him whom that One sent off on a mission."

* Sons- continue to Believe God.*

Have Righteous Judgement

John 7:24 "Judge not according to the appearance, but judge righteous judgment."

Jesus responded to those who were angry about him healing on the Sabbath. Here is a great lesson on moving in the wheel: A man needed to be healed that hour, just as a boy needed to be circumcised on the eighth day, but according to law, one should not work on the Sabbath. As sons, by Grace and Truth, it is also righteous to heal those who are sick or cast down or oppressed by the devil.

Remember Jesus did not come to take away the law but to fulfill it.

Let's Review:

Reflect on what attributes are needed to become complete sons of God. Have you received Him as Lord and Savior? Have you been Born again of Water (been water baptized) and of the Spirit (received the Holy Spirit with evidence of speaking in your heavenly language)? Do you have Grace and Truth operating in you? Has your Zeal for God's house increased? Are you being obedient to His will? Are you believing your Father? And is Grace and Truth helping you make Righteous Judgment?

Remember this is a continuing process.

How encouraging V28b-29 "I do nothing of myself but as my Father hath taught me I speak these things. And he that sent me is with me: the Father hath not left me alone; for I do always those things which please him."

With this encouragement let us continue to look at St. John's gospel in this light of seeing the attributes which will make us mature sons of God - to be able to move in the 'Wheel'.

Continue in the Word

John 8:31, 32 "Then said Jesus to those Jews which believed on him, if ye continue in my word, then are you my disciples indeed; and ye shall know the truth, and the truth shall make you free."

We need to continue studying the Word as a disciplined Son. We will then know the truth and the truth will set us free. Truth here is God's divine revelation - this is freedom! A son needs to know how his father works, therefore we have to know our Father, spend time with Him, work with Him, and discuss things with Him.

In other words, read the manual - the word of God, and phone the manufacturer - pray.

Abide

John 8:34, 35 "Verily, verily, I say unto you, whosoever committeth sin is the servant of sin. And the servant abideth not in the house for ever: but the Son abideth forever."

John 8: 47 "He that is of God heareth God's words: ye therefore hear them not, because ye are not of God."

Abide, means to accept or act in accordance with a rule,

decision or recommendation. Once we have accepted to be the sons of God, we need to 'abide' forever in His house.

There is liberty.

Work While it is Day

John 9:4, 5 "I must work the works of him that sent me, while it is day: the night cometh, when no man can work. As long as I am in the world, I am the light of the world"

A son needs to do what he has been appointed to do, to be about his father's business while it is day, while there is still the light of God.

Understand that our life in Christ is a life time experience and that it is continuous until Christ comes for us. We are the light of the world, and we have to take every opportunity to share this with others so that they can come to God's saving grace.

Give your life:

John 10: 7-18 "I am the good shepherd: the good shepherd, giveth his life for the sheep."

Jesus refers to himself as the 'good shepherd' laying his life down for all sheep who know and hear His voice. As a son we need to protect the people of God, not allowing the devil to steal, kill and destroy the flock. V13"The hireling fleeth, because he is a hireling, and careth not for the sheep." Hirelings allow the 'sheep' to be scattered and killed. Sons care for their household, making sure all are safe and accounted for.

Be Humble

John 13:13-16, V35 Jesus set a standard here washing his disciple's feet. So profound washing his disciple's feet.

John13:13-16 Wuest Translation. "He said to them, do you understand what I have done to you? You call me the teacher and the Lord and well do you say for I Am. Since therefore I, the Lord and Teacher, washed your feet, you also have a moral obligation to be washing one another's feet, for I gave to you an example that just as I did to you, you also should be doing. Most assuredly, I am saying to you, a slave is not greater than his master, nor even one who is sent on a mission greater than the one who sent him. Since you know these things, spiritually prosperous ones you are if you are doing them. V35: In this all shall know that you are my disciples if you constantly have love among one another." As sons of God our heritage is great, we should understand that we are no greater than those who serve. And v16. If we are sent we are no greater than the ones who are sending us.

Be Fruitful and Love

John15: 1-17 Kenneth Wuest translation "I appointed you in order that you might be going away and constantly bearing fruit, and that your fruit might be remaining, in order that whatever you might ask the Father in my name, He may give it to you. These things I am enjoining upon you namely that you should be loving one another with a divine and sacrificial love."

Being fruitful requires us to do some things. It requires a living communion with Jesus as the true vine, it also requires sacrificial love for the brethren.

Sons of God Reproduce Sons of God

Ask

John16:24 "Hitherto have ye asked nothing in my name: ask, and ye shall receive, that your joy may be full."

Several times Jesus talks to his disciples about asking of the father. We can forget or even think we are not worthy of asking, but it is the prerogative of sons to ask their fathers for things, even with abandon (without holding back). Jesus says ask and ye shall receive.

Let's Review:

In our world today, we might have a wrong understanding of the father attribute. As a Father, are you encouraging your children to ask things from you? And do you have the attributes of your Father God to be able to give your children the 'good' things? Be encouraged to develop the attributes of your heavenly Father to be able to give good gifts to your sons.

Speak openly

John: 18:19-20 Wuest Translation. "Then the chief priest asked Jesus concerning his disciples and concerning His teaching Jesus answered him, as for myself, I have spoken openly to the world. I at all times taught in the synagogue and in the temple where all the Jews habitually come together, and in secret I said nothing"

Jesus says some amazing things that we need to take note of. He says. "I spake openly to the world." So he spoke to all. Then he says "I ever taught in the synagogue," this is to the local church. "and in the temple, whither the Jews always resort;" the greater congregation went to hear teaching and to talk about doctrine. "and in secret have I said nothing". Jesus had no hidden agenda, He spoke to everyone.

Jesus had no hidden agenda, what he spoke and discussed was always the truth, we as sons of God should have this same attribute in all that we do and say.

Fulfill your purpose – Son of God

John 21 The disciples go fishing, their former (previous) occupation. They catch nothing. In the morning Jesus appeared on the shore and enquires V5 Wuest "Boys still under instruction, you do not have anything to add to your bread, such as fish, have you?" Jesus directs them to throw their nets on the right side, they catch a very full net, and the net does not break. Jesus already has fish on the fire when they come to shore. Jesus says. V10 "Bring at once some of the fish you have now caught." Then V12 "here have some breakfast." They eat together and afterwards Jesus asks Peter V15, 16, and 17. Do you love me more than these [fish]? Peter's reply is yes all three times. Jesus's instruction is 'Be feeding my little lambs, be shepherding my sheep, be feeding my sheep.

Sometimes we go back to our old job (lifestyle), we lose direction, and we become discouraged.

Jesus's encouragement: -

- He enquires about 'the catch'
- He instructs them on where the fish are.
- He provides some fish

- He invites them to bring some of the fish that they have caught.
- They enjoy the meal together, bread and fish.
- Then Jesus helps Peter affirm (declare) his love for Jesus - Peter's new occupation over the previous occupation of 'fishing'.
- Jesus encourages Peter again to feed and take care of the flock.

Let us attain the attributes of a son of God, and let us continue to mature, for the purpose of Moving with the Spirit in the wheel to 'be shepherding the sheep'.

Jesus's last instruction to Peter was:

Follow me

REVIEW JOHN - SON OF GOD

1. But _____ as received Him, to them gave He _____ to become the sons of God even to them that _____ on His _____.
2. "Our new birth gives us the capacity not to condemn, but through our lives bring people to salvation." __True __False
3. Grace means unmerited _____ _____.
4. Truth means the real or true facts about something. __True __False
5. Christ came to _____ the law of Moses by _____ and _____.
6. "The Son can do _____ of himself, but what he _____ the Father do: for what things _____ he doeth, these also doeth the Son _____."
7. Obedience is not _____. It is the sons good _____ to _____ the Father. _____, _____ and satisfaction are the reward when we move with our _____ in the wheel.
8. Then said Jesus to those Jews which believed on

him, If ye continue in my word, then are ye my disciples indeed;

9. "Jesus answered him, as for myself, I have _____ _____ to the world. I at all times _____ in the synagogue and in the temple where all the Jews habitually come _____, and in _____ I said nothing."

10. What was Jesus' last instruction to Peter? _____ _____. __ go fishing, __ deny me, __ follow me, __ eat breakfast

Chapter 28

LUKE - FACE OF A MAN

Luke's Gospel - the Face of a Man

WE LOOK through Luke's Gospel at attributes that are needed to be the sons of man. We look at Jesus's example in his humanity, how He lived on earth among men. How he did things, what he had to work through, his obedience and his acceptance of his destiny. We will learn how to live as a man on earth.

Enjoy, learn and accept your destiny.

Be Directed

Luke 1:26-37. The Angel Gabriel was sent by God to tell Mary she would conceive, and be the mother of Jesus. Here we see the call of God on Mary's life. The angel came to speak directly to Mary about her destiny, even though Mary was troubled, and fearful she willingly accepted this 'call'. 38 "And Mary said, 'Behold the handmaid of the Lord; be it unto me according to thy word'."

We want to hear from our Maker and accept His desire for our lives to fulfill His purpose on earth. If we are not fully invested in our destiny we will find it very difficult to move in the wheel - it will be in our own strength.

Let us desire to move in the wheel and fulfill God's purpose for our lives. Can you say as Mary said, "Be it unto me, according to thy word?"

Let Others Acknowledge You

Read Luke 1:39-48. When Mary comes to visit Elizabeth, John leapt in Elizabeth's womb, acknowledging Jesus. The spirit in Elizabeth acknowledges Mary and Jesus. V42 "And she spake out with a loud voice, and said, Blessed art thou among woman, and blessed is the fruit of thy womb."

The Holy Spirit moved through Elizabeth, and the baby John leaped in her womb V45 Elizabeth says "And blessed is she that believed: for there shall be a performance of those things which were told her from the Lord." The acknowledgement is of Mary's believing, and her willingness, that the Lord will fulfill destiny through her.

Mary responds V46-48."And Mary said, my soul doth magnify the Lord, and my spirit hath rejoiced in God my Saviour. For he hath regarded the low estate of his handmaiden:" Mary acknowledges the Lord's call upon her and expresses humility.

Review: Are you secure in your destiny? Can you accept acknowledgement from others and not have a false humility?

Can you wait to be acknowledged; to be affirmed by others?

Prophetic Confirmation

Luke 2: 25-38.When Jesus was brought to the temple to be dedicated by his parents, both Simeon, a devout man who was promised by God that he would not die until he saw the Christ, and Anna the prophetess witnessed that Jesus was the one to come (the Messiah).

Prophetic acknowledgement does two things: 1. It confirms our destiny, what we are called to be. 2. It declares our calling to others.

However, be careful that you let the Holy Spirit do the acknowledging. God is the one who knows when the time is right.

Study to be Called

Luke 2:40, 52 "And the child grew, and waxed strong in spirit, filled with wisdom: and the grace of God was upon him." V52 "And Jesus increased in wisdom and stature, and in favour with man and God." Jesus learned natural skills from Joseph, (his trade as a carpenter,) and he also went to the local Synagogue (church) and learned the foundation principles of his faith. Jesus went to Jerusalem and spent time with the scholars which added knowledge and helped mature him.

To be the son of man we have to know our heritage, our calling and we have to know how to live.

Obey the Law of God and the Land

Luke 3:21, 22 "Now when all the people were baptized, it came to pass that Jesus also being baptized, and praying, the heaven was opened, and the Holy Ghost descended in a bodily shape like a dove upon him, and a voice came from heaven, which said, Thou are my beloved Son; in thee I am well pleased."

As a requirement of the law Jesus was baptized. Baptism is to confirm our faith in God and to declare who we belong to. Jesus's Father acknowledges this commitment also declaring that Jesus is His Son. Jesus was obedient to both His Father and the law.

Do Not Fear or Reject Trials

Luke 4: 1-13 Jesus is led into the wilderness by the Holy Spirit. He ate nothing, and He was tempted by the devil for 40 days. The devil challenged Jesus, but because He knew who He was, He responded with the word and authority to the temptation of the devil. Trials help to strengthen us and confirm our position (calling). After this experience...

Luke 4:18-19 when Jesus went to the synagogue and was given the book of Isaiah to read, he reads from chapter 61:1-3: "The spirit of the Lord God is upon me; because the Lord hath anointed me to preach good tidings (the gospel) unto the meek; he hath sent me to bind up the brokenhearted, to proclaim liberty to the captives, and the opening of the prison to them that are bound; To proclaim the acceptable year of the Lord."

Let's Review:

In preparing to move with the Spirit in the wheel we have looked at the following attributes:

Be directed, let others acknowledge you, get prophetic confirmation, study to be called, obey the law of God and the land, do not fear and reject trials and be assured and confident.

Jesus could not have read from the scriptures and declared who He was with confidence without the encouragement from parents, mentors, teachers, and prophets. He also spent time studying the scriptures, (the word of God)

When we move with the Spirit in the wheel, we want to have attributes that will help our fellow man. Our confidence of who we are as sons needs to be sure. We cannot be overcome by doubts, fears, or insecurities when on a mission.

* In the wheel we have to focus on the task at hand, in tune with what the spirit in the wheel is doing.*

What do you look like right now as the son of man, are you taking on His attributes? Are you taking the right steps in your walk in becoming a son of man?

Are you following God's plans to fulfill your destiny?

Many aspects of being a Son of man are similar to the attributes of being a 'Son of God'. While this may seem repetitive, the main point for Luke's gospel is to have attributes to effectively work with man. Remember, we are maturing to move with the Spirit in the wheel.

Move in the Authority

Luke 4:32 "And they were astonished at his doctrine: for his word was with power." When we teach, are others astonished at our doctrine? Is there authority in our words? When Jesus taught His word was with power. Consider your life, what situations might you face where you will need this authority? Do you understand the authority that you have as the son of man?

Here are just a few that were highlighted for me:
We have authority over:

1. Demons - Luke 4:33-35
2. Disease - Luke 4:38, 39
3. Nature Luke: 5:1-11. Although Simon was a fisherman by trade he obeyed when Jesus instructed him to go into the deep and let down the net. Do we trust and obey in the same way even though it is contrary to our natural instincts?
4. Defilement Luke 5:12-14 The leper required more than a healing. His circumstance called for a cleansing.
5. Laws Luke 6:1- Remember Jesus came to fulfill the law. Laws are not meant to bind us or confine - they are meant to free (liberate) us. The religious leaders were addressing the law of not working on the Sabbath. Jesus responds by referring them to the law about gleaning Duet. 23:25

Isaiah 28:9-10 "Whom shall he teach knowledge? And whom shall he make to understand doctrine? Them that are weaned from the milk, and drawn from the breast. For precept must be upon precept, precept upon precept; line upon line, line upon line; here a little, and there a little:" Luke 6:47 "Whosoever cometh to me, and heareth my sayings, and doeth them, I will show you to whom he is like: he is like a man who build an house and digged deep, and laid the foundation on the rock: and when the flood arose, the stream beat vehemently on the house, and could not shake it: for it was founded on a rock. But he that heareth and doeth not, is like a man that without a foundation built a house upon the earth: against which the stream beat vehemently and immediately it fell; and the ruin of that house was great."

Activities

Luke 7:8, 9 The compassion to man is very evident in Luke's gospel. These are some of the things that we as sons do when moving in the wheel.

- Heal the Sick Luke 7:8-10 Jesus was willing to go to a centurion's house to heal his servant and even at the end not go into the house.
- Raise the Dead-Luke 7:11-15. The only motivation was compassion, not for any other reason. There does not need to be a reason to do something good.
- Testimony and Actions to Remove Doubt. Luke 7:18-23 Jesus did not rebuke John or his disciples for wanting reassurance, he continued doing what he came to earth to do thus giving them the assurance.

No pride should come at this point. In humbleness always do what you have been anointed and called to do. Jesus was just doing what he was meant to do. So often we try to make a bigger demonstration, do something extravagant. Why?

And then what did Jesus do?

- Acknowledge others- Luke 7:24-29 Jesus speaks of John and acknowledges him. Jesus quickly disannulled the doubt that people might have had towards John for asking such a question. Let us be quick to acknowledge and authenticate our brothers and sisters.
- Give Wise Counsel – Luke 7:36-50 Jesus goes to Simon's house to eat and there also the woman washes his feet with oil. Oh to get to that place in God where we can without offense use opportunities to give wise council.
- Feed the hungry Luke 9:10-17. Noticing when people need to have food and extending oneself to feed them.
- Follow the Father's will. Luke 9:22-26 For sons to be able to move in the wheel and to be effective, our Father's priority comes first.

* "For the Son of man is not come to destroy men's lives, but to save them" Luke 9:56 *

Martha and Mary

Luke 10: 38 Jesus was at Martha and Mary's house visiting them. It says Martha was encumbered about much serving and was getting overwhelmed. Mary, on the other hand, was at Jesus's feet and this was where the Spirit was moving. Martha also had to be there, but had to provide food. Kenneth Wuest translation: - "But Martha was going around in circles, over-occupied with preparing the meal. And bursting in upon Jesus she assumed a stance over Him and said, "Lord, is it not a concern to you that my sister has let me down to be preparing the meal alone? Speak therefore to her at once that she take hold and do her part with me." And answering, the Lord said to her, "Martha, Martha, you are worried and excited about many things, but of few things there is need, or of one, for Mary chose out for herself the good portion, which is of such a nature that it shall not hastily be snatched away from her."

What activities are you doing that are not necessary (over occupied) and might cause you to miss where the Spirit is going and 'miss' the ride in the wheel because we were 'encumbered with'.

Occupy

Luke 11:20-26 "When a strong man armed keepeth his palace, his goods are in peace: but when a stronger than he shall come upon him, and overcome him, he taketh from him all his armor wherein he trusted, and divideth his spoils. When the unclean spirit is gone out of a man, he walketh through dry places, seeking rest: and finding none, he sayeth I will return unto my house whence I came out. And when he cometh, he findeth it swept and garnished.

Then goeth he and taketh to him seven other spirits more wicked than himself; and they enter in and dwell there: and the last state of the man is worse than the first."

Be sure to take on all attributes of the son of man so that your house will be occupied with the good things "For the Holy Ghost shall teach you in the same hour what you ought to say."

Seek the Kingdom - First

Luke12:14-34. What a great world we could live in if we could grasp this concept and have it working in our lives? V23. "The life is more than meat, and the body is more than raiment". Apply this to your life and let God show you what this really means to you. I think this is a very difficult area to give to our Father and have trust enough that He will fully provide for us. V29 "And seek not what ye shall eat, or what ye shall drink, neither be ye of a doubtful mind." How often do we doubt the Father's provision for us? There are several situations in Luke's gospel where he looks at trusting the Father. How can we overcome in these areas? V31 and 32 tells us how to. "But rather seek ye the kingdom of God; and all these things shall be added unto you. Fear not, little flock; for it is your Father's good pleasure to give you the Kingdom." Do you see this? It is the Father's good pleasure, **His good pleasure!!** Son of man, where is your treasure?

V34. "For where your treasure is, there will your heart be also." Purpose in yourself to 'let God' and experience the incredible freedom of 'all things' being added to you.

Compassion

Luke 13:6-9 "And he answering said unto him, Lord, let it alone this year also, till I shall dig about it, and dung it: and if it bear fruit, well; and if not, then after that thou shall cut it down."

Compassion often requires us to spend our extra time with people to give them a chance to bear fruit.

Develop your compassion, so you can move with God in the wheel to encourage your fellow man to develop fruit.

Count the Cost. Luke 14:25-35

Being a son has a price, but there is security, contentment, peace and joy when we fully embrace our son ship. But, we do need to count the cost, because it does take work and commitment to be a son.

Luke 15: 11-32 the familiar passage about the prodigal son. This son realized the security in being part of his father's house, he was even prepared to be a servant in the household. Also look at the older son's anger, but most importantly see the father's response. Luke 15:31 "And he said unto him, Son, thou art ever with me, and all that I have is thine." Do you realize what is yours as sons? Luke 18:29-30 "And he said unto them, Verily I say unto you, There is a no man that hath left house, or parents, or brethren, or wife, or children, for the kingdom of God's sake, Who shall not receive manifold more in this present time, and in the time to come life everlasting."

Luke 19:10 "For the Son of man is come to seek and to save that which was lost."

Let's Review: Remember that the reason for this study is to move in the wheel when the SPIRIT moves, to minister to man on earth. Embrace all that is a Son so that you can bring those who are lost to salvation?

Watch and Pray Luke 21:34-36

Kenneth Wuest V34: "And take heed to yourselves, lest at any time your hearts be overcharged with surfeiting, and drunkenness, and cares of this life, and so that day come upon you unawares. V36 Watch ye therefore, and pray always, that ye may be accounted worthy to escape all these things that shall come to pass, and to stand before the Son of man." But be circumspect, attentive, ready, in every season being in prayer, in order that you may have sufficient strength to be escaping all these things which are about to take place, and to stand before the son of man."

What love had Jesus for His brothers to continually warn, but most importantly encourage them to watch and pray so that they would not be overcome by the enemy. We need to continually watch and pray.

Be Endued With Power. Luke 24:49

V49 "And, behold, I send the promise of my Father upon you: but tarry ye in the city of Jerusalem, until ye be endued with power from on high."

Sons, do you have the power from on high? We must have all the attributes of the Son to be the sons of man. Will you tarry in the city until you be endued with power from on high? Are you in for the long haul, will you wait until you have been endued? Then you truly will have the ability to move by the Spirit in the wheel.

Wait to be endued with power of the Holy Spirit.

REVIEW: LUKE'S GOSPEL - THE FACE OF A MAN

1. "Behold the handmaid of the Lord; be it _____ _____ _____ to thy word,"
2. "And Jesus increased in _____ and stature and in _____ with man and God,"
3. In Isaiah 28:9 It says whom shall He teach knowledge? And whom shall He teach knowledge? And whom shall He make to understand doctrine?
4. Let us be quick to _____ and _____ our brothers and sisters.
5. Luke 12:31-32 "But rather _____ ye the _____ of God and all _____ _____ shall be _____ unto you. Fear not little flock for it is your Fathers _____ _____ to give you the kingdom."
6. For where your _____ is, there will your _____ be also.
7. Compassion often requires us to spend our _____ _____ with people to give them a chance to _____ _____.
8. But be ye circumspect, _____, ready, in every

season being in _____ in order that you may have sufficient strength.

9. And, behold, I send the promise of my Father upon you: but _____ ye in the city of _____, until ye be _____ with power from _____ _____.

Chapter 29

MATTHEW - FACE OF THE LION

Matthew's Gospel - the Face of a Lion

MATTHEWS'S GOSPEL is written for God's chosen people, the Jews, the Tribe of Judah. In this book our focus is to see how we 'God's Chosen' can come into a greater understanding of Kingdom Living, because of the life that Jesus lived and demonstrated for us. We will also look at some other people who demonstrated effectual living as believers.

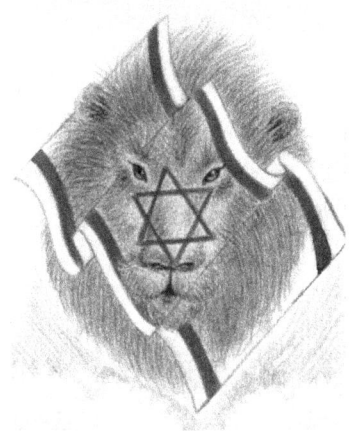

What attributes do we need to have to embrace to move with the Spirit of God in the wheel as God's chosen people?

- The People
- Ordinary man
- Wise Man
- Appointed Man
- Obedience
- Knowledge
- Fulfilling the Law
- Living the Kingdom Way
- Proof of Kingdom Life
- Instructions to the disciples
- Be planted
- Fulfilling the Law
- Do not be deceived
- Know your destiny
- Prayer and Fasting
- Functions to the body of Christ
- Preparation
- Faithful
- Wise
- Remember the Sacrifice
- Fulfill your destiny
- Commission

The People - Ordinary Man

Matthew 1:20-24 Joseph is directed by an angel of the Lord to take Mary as his wife. Joseph did as the angel of the Lord bid him and he called the child's name Jesus when he was born. Joseph was a carpenter, an ordinary person? Yes just a carpenter. Yet Joseph had a conversation with an angel, knew that it was from God, believed the messenger and was willing to obey. What kind of a man was he? Just an ordinary man, a son of David. He was not only willing to take Mary as his wife, bearing the shame that she was already pregnant, but chose to believe the messenger from God and to allow 'History' to unfold. V25 "And knew her not till she had brought forth her firstborn son: and he (Joseph) called his name JESUS."

It was the 'norm' in that time to live a life that was governed by the law (Moses law). Joseph was not a priest, nor a Pharisee, nor an evangelist. He was an ordinary man living a normal life, a carpenter, following the teachings of his heritage.

Wise Man

Matthew 2:1b, 2. "Now when Jesus was born in Bethlehem of Judea in the days of Herod the King, behold, there came wise men from the east to Jerusalem, saying, where is he that is born King of the Jews? For we have seen his star in the east, and are come to worship him."

These wise men (magis) were learned men especially in the study of the stars, they also would have had to have historical knowledge to know about the Christ. Because of their wisdom and knowledge they had followed the star to come and worship the new King.

This was unlike the scholars of Herod's day, who read the prophecies but did not understand the significance of them. Kenneth Wuest translation says "And (Herod) gathering together all the chief priests of the people and the men of the people learned in the sacred scriptures, he went to enquire of them where the Christ should be born. And they said to him, In Bethlehem of Judea, for thus it has been written through the prophet and is on record." Knowledge of history and what has been foretold is an essential part of being able to move in the wheel. As God's chosen we need to get ourselves in position by knowing our (Christian) history, our past and our future. This requires diligent study. 'Why should we do these things' you say? - So when the wheel begins to move we are prepared and we can go where the spirit is moving with the wheel, just like the wise men.

It does not only take knowledge by learning, but a heart that is after the things of God.

Appointed Man

Matthew 3:13, 14, 15 'Then cometh Jesus from Galilee to Jordan unto John, to be baptized of him. But John forbad him, saying, I have need to be baptized of thee, and comest thou to me? And Jesus, answering said unto him, suffer it to be so now: for thus it becometh us to fulfill all righteousness. Then he suffered him.' Both Jesus and John were appointed men, appointed for a specific job.

We see Jesus here determined to fulfill all righteousness, and John consents to the request. Jesus was the son of God. He did not need to be baptized, yet He did this to fulfill all righteousness, and make history.

Let's Review:

Are you living an ordinary believer's life? Could you by your ordinary life as a Christian be in 'line' to have an extraordinary appointment? Like Joseph, Mary or even Elizabeth?

Are you a wise man, knowing the times and positioning yourself to be in the right place to see history made, like the wise men or even Simeon and Anna?

Are you an appointed man moving forward in righteousness to complete the job you have been appointed to do, like John and Jesus?

We will look at the attributes that you will need to enable you to accomplish this.

Obedience

Matthew 2:12 "And being warned of God in a dream that they should not return to Herod, they departed into their own country another way"

V13. "behold the angel of the Lord appeared to Joseph in a dream, saying, Arise, and take the child and his mother, and flee into Egypt, and be there until I bring thee word…, when he arose he took the young child and his mother by night, and departed into Egypt"

Matthew 3:13, 14, 15 "Then cometh Jesus from Galilee to Jordan unto John to be baptized by him. But John forbad him saying I have need to be baptized of thee, and comest thou to me? And Jesus answered and said suffer it to be so now: for thus it becometh us to fulfill all righteousness."

The obedience was without question. The child, Jesus would have been murdered if the wise men had not gone a different way, Joseph would not have had time to escape to

Egypt. If Jesus and John had not obeyed the law to baptize Jesus the confirmation by the Spirit, that Jesus was the son of God could not have happened.

Obedience is an attribute of God's chosen people that is necessary to be able to move in the wheel. Ezekiel 1:12

Knowledge

Matthew 4 Our knowledge of our foundation and biblical history is so important. It gives us a stepping stone into our future. The truths from what was said and done can direct our steps.

Let's look at how Jesus used historical truth after his wilderness experience when the devil tempted him.

Matthew 4:4 "But he answered and said, It is written, Man shall not live by bread alone, but by every word that proceedeth out of the mouth of God." This quote is from Deuteronomy 5 - as a young boy, Jesus would have studied the books of the law. Deuteronomy 8:3c reads: "….that he might make thee know that man doth not live by bread only, but by every word that proceedeth out of the mouth of the Lord doth man live." In Matthew 4:7 Jesus responds: "It is written again, Thou shalt not tempt the Lord your God" (Deuteronomy 6:16) Matthew 4:10 "Then saith Jesus unto him, Get thee hence, Satan; for it is written, Thou shalt worship the Lord thy God, and him only shalt thou serve". Deuteronomy 10:20 "Thou shalt fear the Lord thy God; him shalt thou serve, and to him halt thou cleave, and swear by his name."

Jesus was able, with the knowledge of the Law (His foundation), to make a firm declaration against Satan's temptation using the word of God. Satan knew the word of

God, he was unable to argue with Jesus. The word is truth and power.

Read Deuteronomy 6:12-22. This will give you much insight into the reason we as believers need our history.

Fulfilling the Law

Matthew 5:1-20, V1-16 Jesus is teaching His disciples principles of living, through foundational truths, encouraging the disciples to apply themselves. Then in V17-20 He firmly states that as children of God we need to keep all the law plus love righteousness, the righteousness that fulfills the law. We are looking at a lifestyle – wholly acceptable to God.

V20 "For I say unto you, that except your righteousness shall exceed the righteousness of the scribes and Pharisees, ye shall in no case enter into the kingdom of heaven."

This passage is important to understand, and apply to our lives. It is key to successful ministry to the family of Christ. Jesus assures the disciples that the mosaic laws were still applicable, but righteousness (grace and truth) need to be applied to fulfill the law.

Let's Review:

As a believer, a member of the body of Christ, is your righteousness 'exceeding?'

V 19 says: "but whomever shall do and teach the same shall be called great in the kingdom of heaven."

Assess before God where you are in your life, in obtaining these attributes of a true believer. It does not matter what you do, it matters what type of righteousness you have (the law or the law with grace and truth). Jesus did not come to destroy the law He came to fulfill it.

Do you know the foundation principles of the Christian faith? What does the foundation mean to you?

Our heritage, our history, and our foundation is what makes us who we are. Joseph the father of Jesus, the Wise men, John the Baptist and Jesus knew the foundation of their faith. They were taught as young children at the Synagogue, at the family table every week, and on remembrance days like Passover. This learning and foundation is what enabled them to live their lives to the full and make history.

They listened, they studied, they obeyed and they used the knowledge of their heritage to fulfill their destiny.

Living the Kingdom Way

Matthew Chapter 5 – 7. You will see Jesus teaching on various aspects of kingdom living using the laws written in Exodus, Leviticus, Deuteronomy and Judges. He gives insight to these situations so that the law is not a ritual, but governed by righteousness (grace and mercy) so that there is liberty.

What ways are you still living by the letter of the law? Begin to learn and live by righteous application so that you can move with the Spirit in the wheel. We must 'Come up higher in God's Love' to move in the wheel.

Some examples of the Law and Kingdom thinking.
Matthew 5:21 The law - If you kill you will be judged.

5:22 The fulfillment - If you are angry and say Raca, or say someone is a fool, you will be in danger of going to hell.

5:27 The law- Do not commit adultery.

5:28 The fulfillment- Wuest 'Everyone who is looking at a woman in order to indulge his sexual passion for her, already committed adultery with her in his heart.'

5:33 The law-Don't take an oath on yourself …or of the Lord because it is binding.

5:34, 37 The fulfillment- Don't take an oath by anything or anyone. Let your communication be yea, yea or nay, nay.

5:43 The Law- 'Love thy Neighbor, hate thine enemy.'

5:44 The fulfillment- 'Love your enemy, bless those who curse you, do good to those who hate you, and pray for them which despitefully use you, and persecute you.'

6:1 The religion- When doing alms they sound a trumpet.

6:3, 4 The righteousness- Do your alms in secret, let your father in heaven reward you.

6:5 The Religion- 'Hypocrites pray standing in the synagogue and at the street corners.'

6:6 The Righteousness- 'Enter into thy closet, pray in secret to your Father, who will reward you openly'

Let's Review:

Matthew 19:16-23Jesus was not being unkind to the young man, he was addressing the heart attitude of the man. Wuest translation helps us understand what Jesus was saying "But Jesus says to him, Start following with me as my disciple and continue to do so as a habit of life…," When we make things habits in our lives, this is when there will be fruit of that, good or bad. Our goal in this study is to make our 'habit of life' the Kingdom Life - this is what produces fruit, good fruit.

Allow God to show you the areas in your life that need to be fulfilled and righteous. As you begin to make these attributes, habits in your life, it will become so natural, you will begin to move with the Spirit in the wheel without even thinking about it.

Proof of Kingdom Life

Matthew 7:16, 17, 18 and 21. 'Ye shall know them by their fruits. Do men gather grapes of thorns, or figs of thistles? A good tree cannot bring forth evil fruit, neither can a corrupt tree bring forth good fruit. Not everyone that saith unto me, Lord, Lord, shall enter into the kingdom of heaven; but he that doeth the will of my Father which is in heaven.'

Matthew 9:37,38 "Then saith he unto his disciples, The harvest truly is plenteous, but the labourers are few; pray ye therefore the Lord of the harvest, that he will send forth labourers into the harvest."

WE ARE LOOKING AT WHAT WE PRODUCE THAT COMES FROM the result of being mature sons of the Kingdom of God.

Remember we are developing attributes to make us mature sons of our heritage - the Lion.

The reason is to move in the wheel with the Spirit of the Lord to...

Heal 8:3, 4, 5 The leper asks 'if thou wilt, thou canst make me clean.'...Jesus puts forth his hand and says 'I will, be thou clean.' To bring healing is a product of kingdom living.

Cast out Demons-8:28-33 The authority we have by the

'word' enables us to speak to these spirits and they will obey the word.

Have authority - 8:8. The well-known story of the centurion... "I am not worthy that thou shouldest come under my roof: but speak the word only, and my servant shall be healed. For I am a man under authority, having soldiers under me: and I say to this man go and he goeth...." The centurion recognized that Jesus was under authority.

Have Mercy 9:12, 13 Remember that we are being sent to the lost, those that need a physician.

Go to the lost sheep of Israel- 10:6

Declare that the kingdom of heaven is at hand- 10:7

Heal the sick, cleanse the lepers, and raise the dead, cast out devils-10:8

Remember that the disciple is not above his master, nor the servant above his Lord- V24

Matthew 9:37, 38" Then said he unto his disciples, The Harvest truly is plenteous, but the labourers are few; Pray ye therefore the Lord of the harvest, that he will send forth labourers, into the harvest."

Be Planted

Matthew 13:24-30-parable, V 37-43-explanation.

We so often get caught up in worrying about the wickedness around us that we try to stop it and get uprooted ourselves. As sons of the kingdom we need to be about our Father's business, doing what He has appointed us to do - be planted, grow in God and bear fruit. When the harvest is ready our Father in heaven will come for us, and welcome us home and those who were sown as deception will be condemned.

What does this have to do with the moving of the wheel?

We need to spend time developing our attributes so that we can produce fruit to be part of the good harvest and not contend with the evil that is being sown. Let us be determined to be planted of God. V 14 Jesus say 'let them alone....' We can often spend valuable time trying to destroy evil around us, debating and arguing. It is our job to get our attributes and move with the Spirit in the wheel to produce fruit, so that there can be a harvest.

God is the one who will separate the fruit from the tares when He returns.

Fulfilling the Law

Matthew 15:17, 18 "Do not ye yet understand, that whatsoever entereth in at the mouth goeth into the belly, and is cast out into the draught? But those things which proceed out of the mouth come forth from the heart; and they defile the man."

Law is good - this keeps us safe - but if our hearts are not washed with the word, what we partake of (take into our heart and spirit man) will defile us and that is what will come out of our hearts.

Becoming sons of God requires us to wash ourselves in the word, (take on His attributes), live a lifestyle that others will know who we are- the (Sons of God).

Do not be Deceived

Matthew 16: 1-12

The religious leaders were tempting Jesus, asking for a sign from heaven. He cautions his disciples to not be blinded by the (false) teaching of the Pharisees and Sadducees, the religiousness of their teaching.

Know your Destiny

Matthew 16:21, 22, 23 "From that time forth began Jesus to shew unto his disciples, how that he must go unto Jerusalem, and suffer many things of the elders and chief priests and scribes, and be killed, and be raised again the third day." When Peter rebukes him, Jesus's response is-V23 "Get thee behind me, Satan: thou art an offence unto me: for thou savourest not the things that be of God, but those that be of men."

Jesus knew his destiny, therefore he was able to purpose to fulfill it.

* Imagine what would have happened if Jesus had got out of the wheel at that point? *

Let's Review:

Do you know your destiny? Whether you are an ordinary man, a wise man or an appointed man, look at where you are in your life with the destiny God has put before you. Know your destiny so you can fulfill it and not be derailed. Remember you are getting ready to ride in the wheel with God.

Prayer and Fasting

Matthew: 17:20, 21 "Howbeit this kind goeth not out but by prayer and fasting."

This particular response comes after the disciples are

not able to rebuke the devil out of a child, Jesus said the disciples were of 'little faith.' The attribute of praying and fasting is what increases faith and what is necessary for certain 'kinds' of demonic forces.

Remember we are looking at our attributes in Matthews's gospel so that we can move in the wheel to serve our family, the body of Christ.

Functions to the Body of Christ

Matthew 20:25, 26, 27, 28 "But Jesus called them unto him, and said, 'Ye know that the princes of the Gentiles exercise dominion over them, and they that are great exercise authority upon them. But it shall not be so among you: whosoever will be great among you, let him be your minister; and whosoever will be chief among you, let him be your servant; even as the Son of man came not to be ministered unto, but to minister, and to give his life a ransom for many.'"

Read through Chapters 18, 19, 20 and 21.

A few examples;

- Take time to find the lost and rejoice Matthew 18:13
- When brothers trespass (commit an act of sin) Matthew: 18:15 -17
- Coming into agreement in my name Matthew: 18:18, 19, 20
- Principle of forgiving. Matthew: 18. 21-35

Preparation

Matthew 22:11, 12 "And when the king came in to see the guests, he saw there a man which had not on a wedding garment: And he saith unto him, Friend, how camest thou in thither not having a wedding garment? And he was speechless."

After the wedding guests were called there was still room at the banquet, because some were too busy attending to 'life'.

The call to salvation is to all those who are destitute and lost, even from the highways and byways.

Jesus invites all that are lost, when we accept the invitation (of salvation), we must prepare ourselves (as a bride) for the coming of the 'bridegroom'.

Faithful

Matthew 24:45, 46, 47 "Who then is a faithful and wise servant, whom his lord hath made ruler over his household, to give them meat in due season? Blessed is that servant, whom his lord when he cometh shall find so doing. Verily I say unto you, that he shall make him ruler over all his goods."

When the lord of the house is able to leave the responsibility of the family to a faithful and wise servant and know that his household will be taken care of, this is a mature son. Faithfulness is a key attribute moving in the wheel.

Wise

Matthew 25: 1-13 and 14-30 Righteous wisdom is also a key attribute to our goals in life. Like the examples of the wise virgins and the servants who were given talents. If we were to wait or try and help others who are not making an effort themselves, we could find ourselves not ready to be at the wedding feast or not able to reproduce what God has appointed for us to do. The result is not being able to be present with God.

Remember the Sacrifice

Matthew 26:26-28 When we have a meal together as believers we are instructed to break bread to remember Jesus's sacrifice. This will encourage us to get the attributes that we need, that we are bonded together, and remember what the purpose of Jesus's death was for.

Fulfill your Destiny

Matthew 26:51-54. It is important to fight the correct battle and not go ahead of the wheel. Jesus encourages everyone to allow the fulfillment of their destiny. V54 "But how then shall the scriptures be fulfilled, that thus it must be."

Commission

Matthew 28:19, 20 "Go ye therefore, and teach all nations, baptizing them in the name of the Father, and of the Son, and of the Holy Ghost: teaching them to observe all things whatsoever I have commanded you: and lo, I am with you always, even unto the end of the world.

This is the purpose!!!! To be commissioned. All the attributes of Christ, as the servant –the ox, as the son of God – the eagle, as the son of man – the man, and our heritage as God's chosen – the Lion is what we need to have to be able to move with God by the Spirit in the wheel, when we are commissioned.

ENJOY THE RIDE

REVIEW: MATTHEW - FACE OF THE LION

1. It does not only take _____ by learning, but a _____ that is after the things of God.
2. Are you an _____ man moving in _____ to complete the job you have been appointed to do?
3. _____ is an attribute of God's _____ people that is necessary to be able to move in the wheel.
4. Satan, when the _____ of God, he was unable to argue with Jesus. The word is _____ and power.
5. Jesus assured His disciples that the mosaic laws were still applicable but _____ _____ _____ need to be _____ to fulfill the law.
6. They listened, they _____, they _____, they used the knowledge of their heritage to fulfill their destiny.
7. It is our job to get our _____ and move with the Spirit in the wheel to _____ fruit, so that there can be a _____.
8. Becoming a son of God requires us to _____ live a lifestyle that others will know. __a. wash ourselves in the word who we are - sons of God,

__b. live a lifestyle that others will know who we are __c. kick back and leave it up to God, __both a and b

9. Prayer and fasting are kingdom functions that we may need to be able to overcome demonic forces. __True __False

10. "_____ ye therefore, and _____ all nations, _____ them in the name of the Father, and of the _____, and of the _____ Ghost: _____ _____ to observe all things whatsoever I have _____ you: and, lo, I _____ with you alway, even unto the end of the world. Amen."

REVIEW KEY: EZEKIEL'S WHEEL

Revelation of Jesus Christ

1. servant, Son of God, Son of Man, King, Son of God, human
2. in us, power, glory
3. forward, went, turned not
4. T
5. permitting God to totally train them by the Spirit of the Lord
6. Holy Spirit
7. servant, pride
8. Joy, Righteousness, Love, Peace, Holiness
9. F
10. T
11. received the revelation, power of the Spirit, Jesus, speaking
12. T
13. delight, thyself, feed, heritage, mouth
14. F

15. preparing, mighty, need, fullness, obey, fullness, father
16. hate, anger, pride

Mark - Face of the Ox

1. great while, with, prayer, direction, master, move, wheel
2. disciples, direction, Father, each
3. serve, put before us
4. T
5. not, ministered, ransom
6. forgive, ought
7. T
8. Spirit, crowd, majority
9. attributes, learn
10. 10. F

John - Son of God

1. as many, power, believe, name
2. T
3. divine assistance
4. T
5. fulfill, grace, truth
6. nothing, seeth, so ever, likewise
7. bondage, pleasure, obey
8. believed, continue, disciples, know, truth
9. spoken, openly, taught, together, secret
10. follow me

Luke's Gospel - the Face of a Man

1. unto, me, according
2. wisdom, God
3. Those who are weaned from the milk
4. acknowledge, authenticate
5. seek, kingdom, these, things, added, good, pleasure
6. treasure, heart
7. extra time, develop fruit
8. attentive, prayer
9. tarry, Jerusalem, endued, on, high

Matthew - Face of the Lion

1. knowledge, heart
2. appointed, righteousness
3. Obedience, chosen
4. word, truth
5. grace, and, truth, applied
6. studied, obeyed
7. attributes, produce, harvest
8. both a and b
9. True
10. Go, teach, baptizing, Son, Holy, teaching them, commanded, am

ABOUT ISAIAH 58 MOBILE TRAINING INSTITUTE

Thank you to those who have:
1 Corinthians 3:6-8 (NLV)
"I planted the seed. Apollos watered it, but it was God Who kept it growing. This shows that the one who plants or the one who waters is not the important one. God is the important One. He makes it grow. The one who plants and the one who waters are alike. Each one will receive his own reward."

Isaiah 58 Mobile Training Institute website:
is58mti.org

www.ingramcontent.com/pod-product-compliance
Lightning Source LLC
Chambersburg PA
CBHW071311110526
44591CB00010B/861